PEARSON LANGUAGE CENTRAL for MATH

PEARSON

Glenview, Illinois • Boston, Massachusetts • Chandler, Arizona • Upper Saddle River, New Jersey

Language Central for Math
Fitchburg Public Schools Curriculum Project Team

Principal Author
Patricia Page Aube

Contributing Authors
Grades 3–5
Lee Cormier
Amy Dessureau
Helen Frerichs
Susan Hanno
Carmelita Hoffmann
Kelly Waples McLinden
Cynthia Rosancrans
Eileen Shireman

Project Director
Bonnie Baer-Simahk

Technical Assistance
Richard Lavers

Sponsor
Massachusetts Department of Elementary and Secondary Education's (ESE) Office of English Language Acquisition, 2009.

This work is protected by United States copyright laws and is provided *solely for the use of teachers and administrators* in teaching courses and assessing student learning in their classes and schools. Dissemination or sale of any part of this work (including the World Wide Web) will destroy the integrity of the work and is *not* permitted.

Cover Art: Lorena Alvarez

Copyright © 2011 by Pearson Education, Inc., or its affiliates. All rights reserved. Printed in the United States of America. This publication is protected by copyright, and permission should be obtained from the publisher prior to any prohibited reproduction, storage in a retrieval system, or transmission in any form or by any means, electronic, mechanical, photocopying, recording, or likewise. The publisher hereby grants permission to reproduce these pages, in part or in whole, for classroom use only, the number not to exceed the number of students in each class. For information regarding permission(s), write to Pearson School Rights and Permissions Department, One Lake Street, Upper Saddle River, New Jersey 07458.

Pearson® is a trademark, in the U.S. and/or in other countries, of Pearson plc, or its affiliates.

ISBN-13: 978-0-13-317290-4
ISBN-10:   0-13-317290-2

How to Use Language Central for Math

This book will help you **think, talk,** and **write** about what you are learning in your math class. Every lesson has 4 pages to help you learn the language needed to succeed in math.

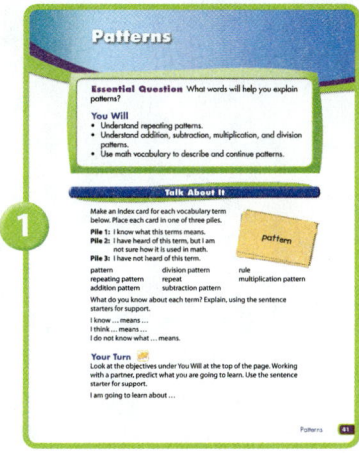
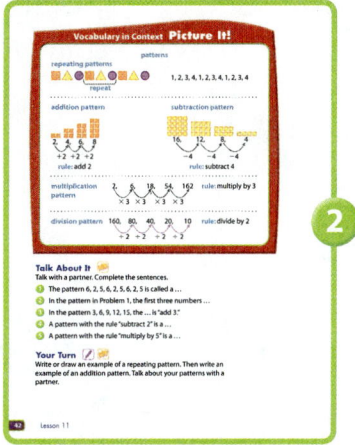
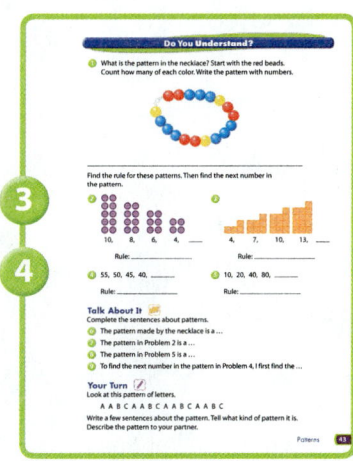

1. Activities connect what you know with what you will learn. Look for the **blue bar** on the first page.

2. Vocabulary terms are shown with pictures to help you learn what they mean. Look for the **red box** on the second page.

3. Look for clues to help you know when to write an answer and when to speak an answer.

4. Practice the skills you learn in your math class.

CONTENTS
Grade 4

Lesson 1: Place Value **1**
Lesson 2: Comparing and Ordering Numbers **5**
Lesson 3: Addition and Subtraction **9**
Lesson 4: Multiplication **13**
Lesson 5: Division **17**
Lesson 6: Whole-Number Operations **21**
Lesson 7: Factors and Multiples..................... **25**
Lesson 8: Decimal Notation **29**
Lesson 9: Estimation **33**
Lesson 10: Fractions and Decimals **37**
Lesson 11: Patterns **41**
Lesson 12: Patterns in Tables **45**
Lesson 13: Variables and Equations **49**
Lesson 14: Lines and Angles........................ **53**
Lesson 15: Shapes **57**
Lesson 16: Transformations and Symmetry **61**
Lesson 17: Measurement **65**
Lesson 18: Converting Units of Measure **69**
Lesson 19: Perimeter and Area **73**
Lesson 20: Time **77**
Lesson 21: Collecting and Organizing Data **81**
Lesson 22: Representing Data...................... **85**

Resources **89**

Place Value

Essential Question What vocabulary terms should you know and use when you discuss place value?

You Will
- Represent numbers through 999,999.
- Use standard form, word form, and expanded form to write numbers.
- Use math vocabulary to express place-value ideas.

Talk About It

Rate these mathematical terms according to the following scale.

1. I do not know this term.
2. I have heard this term, but I do not know how to use it in math.
3. I understand this term and I know how to use it in math.

_____ place value   _____ digit
_____ ones   _____ tens
_____ hundreds   _____ thousands
_____ ten thousands   _____ hundred thousands
_____ expanded form   _____ standard form
_____ value   _____ word form

Explain what you know about each term, using the sentence starters.

I do not know what … means.
I think … means …
I know … means … in math.

Your Turn

Look at the objectives under You Will at the top of the page. Working with a partner, predict what you are going to learn. Use the sentence starter for support.

I am going to learn about …

Vocabulary in Context Picture It!

digits   0 1 2 3 4 5 6 7 8 9

place value

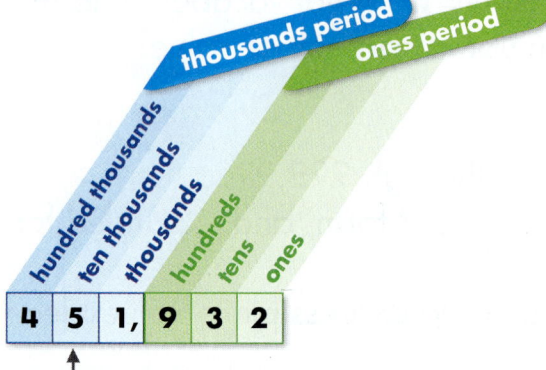

The **value** of the 5 in 451,932 is 50,000.

standard form   451,932

expanded form   400,000 + 50,000 + 1,000 + 900 + 30 + 2

word form   four hundred fifty-one thousand, nine hundred thirty-two

Talk About It
Talk with a partner to complete the sentences.

1. In the number 451,932, the 3 is in the … place.
2. The value of the 7 in 701,254 is …
3. 6,000 + 300 + 40 + 5 is written in …
4. The expanded form of a number shows each digit's …

Your Turn
Write a 5-digit number. Use all different digits. Write the place value of each digit. Tell your number to a partner. Tell the value of each digit.

Lesson 1

Do You Understand?

The numbers in the map are the populations of some cities in the United States. Write each population in the place-value chart.

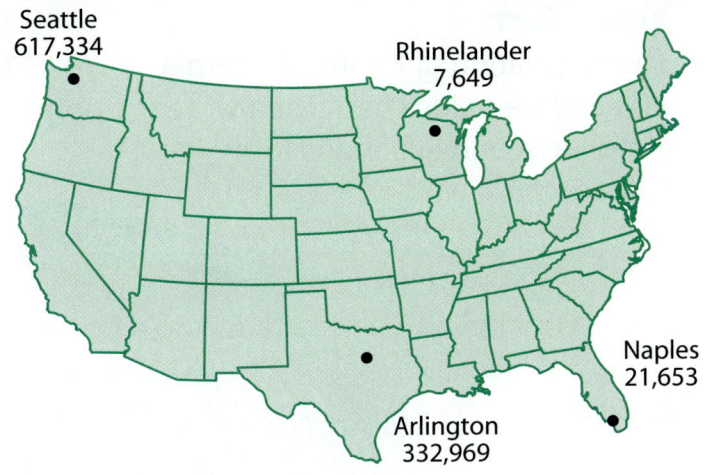

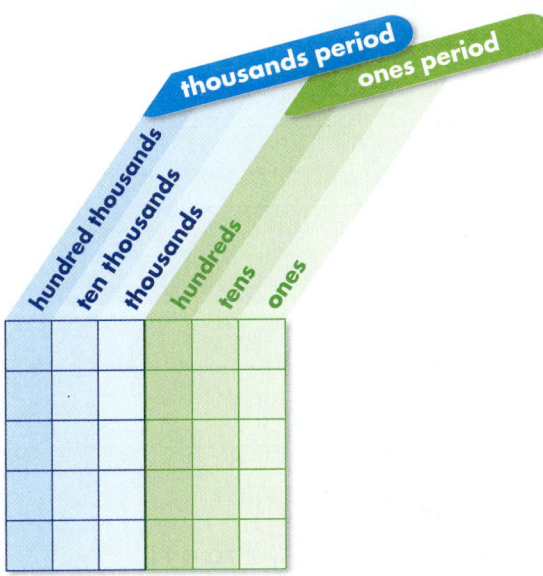

Talk About It

How can you describe these numbers? Complete the sentences.

1. The number 7,649 has four …

2. The number 21,653 has a 1 in the … place.

3. In the number 617,334, the … of the 7 is 7,000.

4. "Three hundred thirty-two thousand, nine hundred sixty-nine" is the … for the number 332,969.

Your Turn

Write a 6-digit number in the place-value chart above. Say the word form of your number to your group. Then tell the value of each digit.

Place Value

Think, Talk, and Write

Your Turn
The population of Fresno, California, is 479,921. Write the population in the place-value chart. Then write the population in standard form, word form, and expanded form.

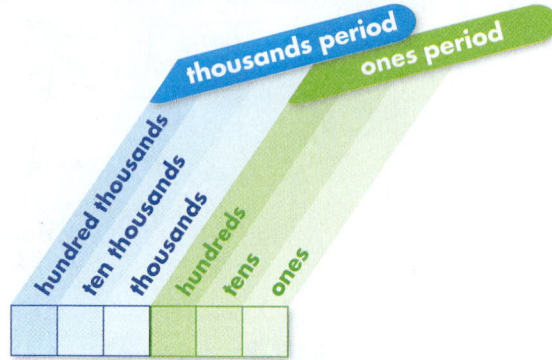

Standard form: _____

Word Form: _____

_____

Expanded Form: _____

_____

Talk and Write About It
Complete the sentences about the number 479,921.

Vocabulary

| ones | digits | tens | ten thousands |
| value | hundreds | thousands | hundred thousands |

① The 7 is in the _____ place.

② 400,000 is the _____ of the 4.

③ The number has six _____ .

Produce Language
Explain how knowing about place value helps you to read and write numbers. Use as many vocabulary terms as you can.

Lesson 1

Comparing and Ordering Numbers

Essential Question How do you use words and symbols (<, >, =) to compare and order numbers?

You will
- Use the symbols <, >, and = to compare and order numbers.
- Use math vocabulary to compare and order numbers.

Talk About It

Rate these mathematical terms according to the following scale.

① I do not know this term.

② I have heard this term, but I do not know how to use it in math.

③ I understand this term and know how to use it in math.

_____ compare   _____ is greater than
_____ equals (is equal to)   _____ is less than
_____ least   _____ order
_____ symbols   _____ greatest

Explain what you know about these terms, using the sentence starters.

I know … means … in math.
I think … means …
I do not know what … means.

Your Turn

Look at the objectives listed under You Will at the top of the page. Working with a partner, predict what you are going to learn. Use the sentence starter for support.

I am going to learn about …

Vocabulary in Context Picture It!

compare Tell how things are the same or different.

equals The same amount as

12 + 4   **equals**   16.
12 + 4   **is equal to**   16.
12 + 4   =   16

greater Bigger

15 **is greater than** 13.
15   >   13

less Smaller

24 **is less than** 31.
24   <   31

symbols   **numbers in order**
  =   >   <   4, 11, 16, 22, 50
                            ↑   ↑
                          least   **greatest**

Talk About It

Talk with a partner to complete the sentences.

1. 134 … 88.
2. 50 + 50 … 100.
3. 100 < 213 means one hundred … two hundred thirteen.
4. The numbers 6, 11, 18, 37 are written in order from least to …

Your Turn

Think about the new vocabulary terms and symbols. Write a number sentence for each of the symbols =, <, and >.

Lesson 2

Do You Understand?

The table shows the number of DVDs rented during three days.

Day	Number Rented
Friday	3,302
Saturday	2,382
Sunday	1,968

You can use words and symbols to compare the number of DVDs rented on Sunday to the number of DVDs rented on Saturday.

Words: 1,968 is less than 2,382.

Symbols: 1,968 < 2,382

1. Compare the number of DVDs rented on Saturday to the number of DVDs rented on Friday.

   Words: _____

   Symbols: _____

2. Compare the number of DVDs rented on Friday to the number of DVDs rented on Sunday.

   Words: _____

   Symbols: _____

3. Going from top to bottom, the numbers in the table are written from greatest to _____.

Talk About It

Talk with a partner about each symbol.

4. The symbol < means …

5. The symbol = means …

6. The symbol > means …

Your Turn

Choose any two numbers from the box. Compare them. Choose any three numbers in the box. Write them from least to greatest. Talk about your work with a group.

823	72
155	369
2,400	1,027

Comparing and Ordering Numbers

Think, Talk, and Write

Your Turn
The table shows how many pop, rock, and rap CDs were sold at a music store.

Kind of CD	Number Sold
Pop	5,066
Rock	7,921
Rap	4,370

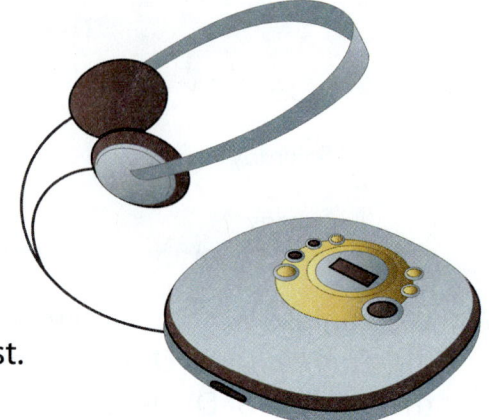

Write the numbers in order from least to greatest.

_____ , _____ , _____

Talk and Write About It
Complete the sentences about the numbers in your table.

Vocabulary

| compare | is greater than | equals | is less than |
| is equal to | order | least | greatest |

1. The number of pop CDs _____ the number of rap CDs.

2. The number of rap CDs _____ the number of rock CDs.

3. The number of rock CDs _____ the number of pop CDs.

4. In the table, 7,921 is the _____ number.

5. The number of rap CDs _____ 4,370.

Produce Language
Write about what you have learned about comparing and ordering numbers. Give examples. Use the vocabulary terms and symbols.

Lesson 2

Addition and Subtraction

Essential Question What words and symbols do you need to know in order to talk about addition and subtraction?

You Will
- Add two numbers with and without regrouping.
- Subtract two numbers with and without regrouping.
- Use symbols to write addition and subtraction sentences.
- Use math vocabulary to express addition and subtraction concepts.

Talk About It

Make an index card for each vocabulary term below. Place each card in one of three piles.

Pile 1 I know what this term means.
Pile 2 I have heard of this term, but I am not sure how it is used in math.
Pile 3 I have not heard of this term.

add	equals	difference
addition	total	operation
addends	subtract	regroup
sum	subtraction	symbols
plus	minus	

What do you know about each term? Explain, using the sentence starters for support.

I know … means …
I think … means …
I do not know what … means.

Your Turn

Look at the objectives listed under You Will at the top of the page. Working with a partner, predict what you are going to learn. Use the sentence starter for support.

I am going to learn about …

Addition and Subtraction

Vocabulary in Context Picture It!

add

addends **sum**

addition sentence: $8 + 2 = 10$

plus **equals**

The **total** amount is 10.

subtract

subtraction sentence: $9 - 3 = 6$

minus **difference**

Addition and subtraction are two kinds of **operations**.

symbols $+$ $-$ $=$

regroup

$$\begin{array}{r}\overset{1}{4}\,7\\ +\,3\,8\\ \hline 8\,5\end{array}$$

15 ones = 1 ten 5 ones

$$\begin{array}{r}\overset{8\,12}{\cancel{9\,2}}\\ -\,1\,7\\ \hline 7\,5\end{array}$$

9 tens 2 ones = 8 tens 12 ones

Talk About It

Talk with a partner. Complete the sentences.

1. To find the sum of two numbers, you …
2. In $12 + 16 = 28$, the numbers 12 and 16 are called the …
3. You subtract two numbers to find their …
4. 10 plus 5 … 15.
5. When adding, sometimes you need to move 10 ones to the tens place to …

Your Turn

Write a number sentence that shows the sum of two numbers. Label the sum.

Write a number sentence that shows the difference between two numbers. Label the difference.

Describe your number sentences to a partner. Use as many vocabulary terms as you can.

Lesson 3

Do You Understand?

The number of children who play on sports teams at the park is shown below.

Baseball
275 children

Football
324 children

Soccer
358 children

Basketball
158 children

Complete each problem.

1 How many children play football and soccer in all?

$$\begin{array}{r} 324 \\ +358 \\ \hline \end{array}$$

In all, _____ children play football and soccer.

2 How many more children play baseball than basketball?

$$\begin{array}{r} 275 \\ -158 \\ \hline \end{array}$$

_____ more children play baseball than basketball.

Talk About It

Talk with a partner about addition and subtraction. Complete the sentences.

3 To find the total number of children who play two sports, I …

4 To find the difference, I …

5 To subtract the ones in 275 minus 158, I need to …

Your Turn

Write two numbers. Each one should have three or four digits. Find the sum of your numbers. Then find the difference of your numbers. Tell a partner how you found each answer.

Addition and Subtraction

Think, Talk, and Write

Your Turn

Four children collect baseball cards.

Denise
360 cards

Julio
195 cards

Inez
234 cards

Henry
406 cards

1. Choose two of the children shown. Find the total number of baseball cards.

2. Choose two other children. Find the difference in the number of baseball cards.

Talk and Write About It

Complete the sentences about addition and subtraction.

Vocabulary

add	operation	addition	regroup
subtract	difference	subtraction	sum
plus	addend	total	equals

3. When I subtract, I am finding the _____ .

4. If the problem has a plus sign, I am using _____ .

5. The symbol = means _____ .

6. Breaking tens into ones is one way to _____ .

Produce Language

Write a set of instructions about how you find sums and differences. For support, use the vocabulary cards you made at the beginning of the lesson.

Lesson 3

Multiplication

Essential Question What words and symbols should you use when you discuss multiplication?

You Will
- Use an array to model multiplication.
- Use math vocabulary to express multiplication concepts.

Talk About It

Make an index card for each vocabulary term below.

Place each card in one of three piles.

Pile 1 I know what this term means.
Pile 2 I have heard this term, but I am not sure how it is used in math.
Pile 3 I do not know this term.

multiply	multiplication
array	factor
product	times
multiple	row
column	

Explain what you know about these terms, using the sentence starters.

I know … means … in math.
I think … means …
I do not know what … means.

Your Turn

Look at the objectives listed under You Will at the top of the page. Working with a partner, predict what you are going to learn. Use the sentence starter for support.

I am going to learn about …

Vocabulary in Context Picture It!

multiply

$$\begin{array}{r} 2 \\ \times\, 4 \\ \hline 8 \end{array}$$

times → ×4 → factors
product ↑ (pointing to 8)

array

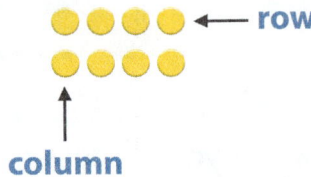

← row
↑ column

2 (rows) × 4 (columns) = 8

multiplication sentence

2 × 4 = 8

multiples of 4

4, 8, 12, 16, …

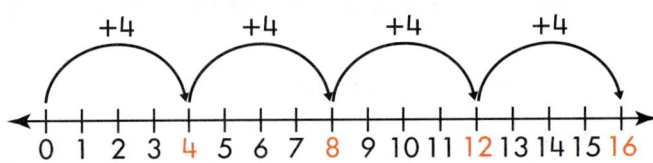

Talk About It

Talk with a partner to complete the sentences.

1. The numbers multiplied to give a product are the …
2. The answer in multiplication is the …
3. When you see the × symbol, you say …
4. A model with rows and columns is an …
5. 6, 12, 18, 24, 30, 36 are … of 6.

Your Turn

Think about the new vocabulary terms.

- Write a multiplication sentence. Circle the factors. Underline the product.
- Choose any number from 2 to 9. List its first three multiples.

Share your answers with a partner.

Lesson 4

Do You Understand?

Students are putting on a play. They will set up 3 rows of chairs with 14 chairs in a row. That arrangement forms the array pictured below.

$3 \times 14 =$ total number of chairs

To find the product, break up the array to make easier problems. Fill in the missing numbers.

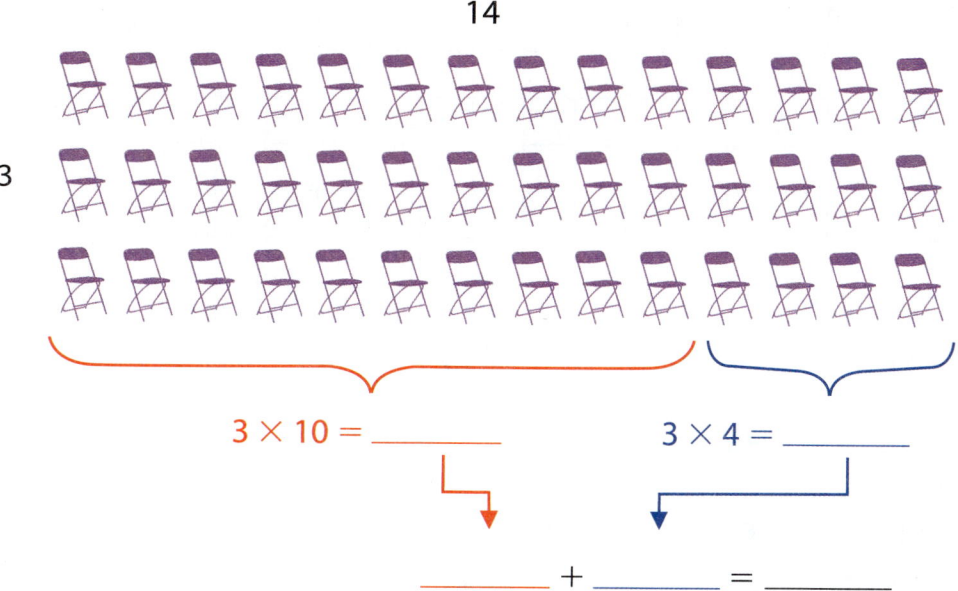

$3 \times 10 =$ _____ $3 \times 4 =$ _____

_____ + _____ = _____

The students will use _____ chairs.

Talk About It

Use multiplication terms to describe the problem. Complete the sentences.

1. A set of rows and columns is called an …
2. In the multiplication sentence $3 \times 14 = 42$, the … are 3 and 14.
3. In the multiplication sentence $3 \times 14 = 42$, the … is 42.

Your Turn

Write a few sentences that explain how you found the total number of chairs. Share your ideas with a group.

Multiplication

Think, Talk, and Write

Your Turn
How many chairs would the students use if they make 6 rows with 16 chairs in each row? Draw your array on the grid below.

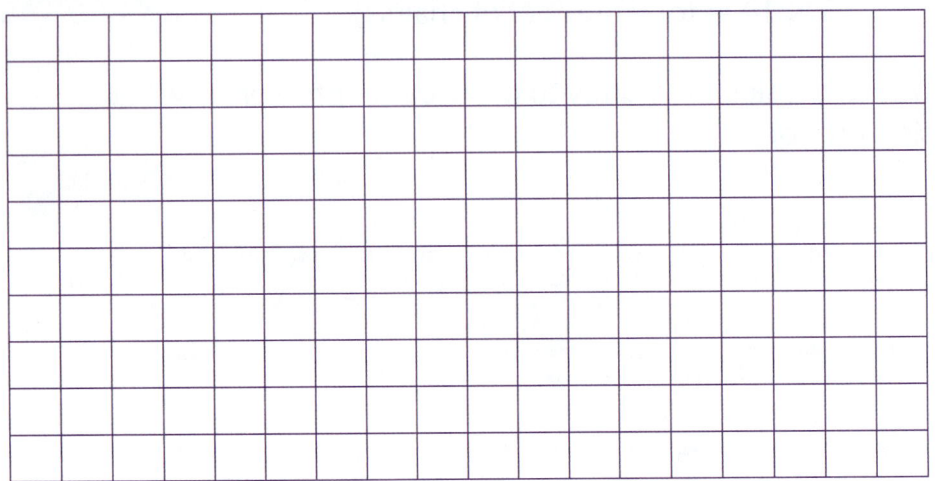

Write a multiplication sentence for your array.

_____ × _____ = _____

The students would use _____ chairs.

Talk and Write About It
Complete the sentences about the problem.

Vocabulary: multiply, multiplication, array, factors, product, columns, multiple, times

1. My array has 6 rows and 16 _____ .
2. The number of rows and the number of columns in the array are the _____ in my multiplication sentence.
3. The answer in my multiplication sentence is called the _____ .

Produce Language
Write about how to use arrays to show multiplication. For support, use the vocabulary cards you made at the beginning of the lesson.

Lesson 4

Division

Essential Question What vocabulary terms and symbols should you use when you discuss division?

You Will
- Use division to solve problems.
- Use symbols to write division problems.
- Use math terms to talk about division.

Talk About It

Look at the list of terms below. In the first two columns of the chart, write terms you **know** or **want** to know more about.

divide	quotient	dividend
division	fact family	divisor
divided by	divisible	remainder

Know	Want	Learned

What do you know about each term you wrote in the chart? Explain. Use the sentence starters for help.

I know … means …
I think … means …

Your Turn

Look at the objectives listed under You Will at the top of the page. Working with a partner, predict what you will learn. Use the sentence starter below.

I am going to learn about …

Vocabulary in Context Picture It!

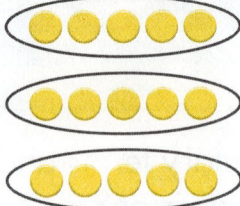

divide

division sentence:

dividend → **divisor**
$$15 \div 5 = 3$$
divided by ↓ ↳ **quotient**

$$5\overline{)15}^{\,3}$$

15 is **divisible** by 5.
It has no remainder.

$$5\overline{)17}^{\,3R2} \leftarrow \text{remainder}$$

17 is *not* **divisible** by 5.
It has a remainder.

fact family $3 \times 5 = 15$ $15 \div 5 = 3$
         $5 \times 3 = 15$ $15 \div 3 = 5$

Talk About It

Talk with a partner to complete the sentences.

1. In $18 \div 6 = 3$, the number 3 is the …
2. $6 \div 2 = 3$ and $2 \times 3 = 6$ are in the same …
3. Six is … by 2.
4. In $37 \div 5$, the … is 2.

Your Turn

Write the rest of the fact family for $8 \times 7 = 56$. Label the parts of one of the division sentences. Use as many vocabulary terms as you can. Describe your answers with a partner.

Lesson 5

Do You Understand?

There are 14 markers.

Divide the markers into 3 equal groups.
Draw them in the cups.
Draw any extras in the box.

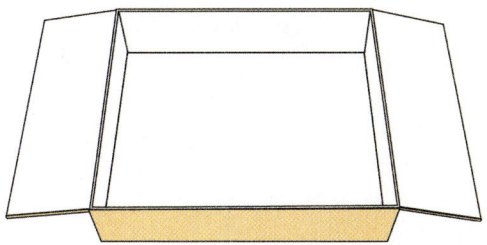

Markers in each cup: _____   Markers left over: _____

So 14 ÷ 3 is _____ with a remainder of _____ .

Fill in the missing numbers.

```
  □R□
3)14
 -12
   2
```

Talk About It

Talk with a partner about division. Complete the sentences.

1. I can make equal groups using …
2. When I divide, the answer is the …
3. Fourteen is not divisible by 3, because there is a …
4. The ÷ symbol and the ⟌ symbol both mean …

Your Turn

What does *divisible* mean? Draw a picture and write a few sentences.
Use the sentence starter for support. Share your paper with a partner.

A number is divisible if …

Division   19

Think, Talk, and Write

Your Turn
Draw a picture of how to divide your class into groups of 4. Complete the division problem.

Number of students in class: _____

There are _____ groups.

4)‾‾‾‾‾

There are _____ students left over.

Talk and Write About It
Complete the sentences about the groups you made.

Vocabulary

| divide | division | divisible | dividend |
| quotient | remainder | fact family | divided by |

1. To make groups of 4, I had to _____ .
2. In my division problem, the number of students in the class is the _____ .
3. The number of leftover students is the _____ .
4. If there is no remainder, the number of students is _____ by 4.

Produce Language
Write the terms you learned about in this lesson in the third column of the chart on page 17. Write what you know about these terms. Use sentence starters from throughout the lesson for support.

20 Lesson 5

Whole-Number Operations

Essential Question What vocabulary terms do you need to understand when you solve problems?

You Will
- Add, subtract, multiply, and divide to solve story problems.
- Use math vocabulary to talk about solving problems.

Talk About It

Copy each term from Vocabulary in Context on a card. As your teacher reads each term, create three piles of cards.

Pile 1 I know what this term means.
Pile 2 I have heard of this term, but I am not sure how it is used in math.
Pile 3 I have not heard of this term.

Explain what you know about these terms, using the sentence starters.

I know … means …
I think … means …
I do not know what … means.

Your Turn
Look at the objectives listed under You Will at the top of the page. Working with a partner, predict what you are going to learn. Use the sentence starter for support.

I am going to learn about …

Whole-Number Operations   21

Vocabulary in Context   Picture It!

whole numbers   2, 8, 17, 104

add

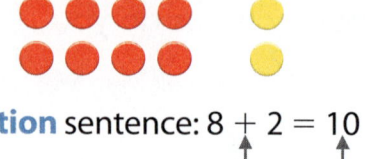

addition sentence: 8 + 2 = 10
                              ↑   ↑
                            plus   sum

subtract

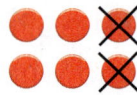

subtraction sentence: 6 − 2 = 4
                                  ↑   ↑
                              minus   difference

multiply

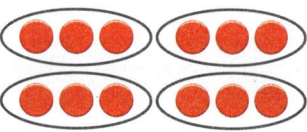

multiplication sentence:

4 × 3 = 12
    ↑   ↑
times   product

divide

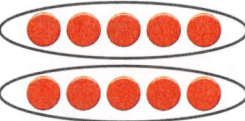

division sentence:

10 ÷ 5 = 2
    ↑   ↑
divided by   quotient

2R1
5)11
      ↑
remainder

operations + − × ÷

Talk About It

Talk with a partner to complete the sentences.

1. 8, 41, and 170 are all …
2. To find how many more things are in one group than another, use …
3. If a number divides evenly, there is no …
4. If things are in equal groups, you can … to find the total number.

Your Turn

Write a number sentence. Tell your partner about it. Use as many vocabulary terms as you can.

Lesson 6

Do You Understand?

Read the problem. Draw a picture. Decide whether you should add, subtract, multiply, or divide. Write a number sentence and give the answer. The first problem is started for you.

Problem	Picture	Number Sentence and Answer
1 A fourth-grade class has 92 students. 47 are girls. How many are boys?	92 students / 47 girls ? boys	92 − 47 = _____ _____ boys
2 The Art Club is making 15 banners. Four gold stars are needed for each one. How many gold stars does the Art Club need?		
3 A gym class has 42 students. How many teams of 6 can be made?		
4 There are 240 blue balloons and 175 red balloons at the school picnic. In all, how many balloons are there?		

Talk About It

Complete the sentences to tell about the problems.

5 To solve Problem 1, I needed to …

6 To solve Problem 2, I needed to …

7 To solve Problem 3, I needed to …

8 To solve Problem 4, I needed to …

Your Turn

Choose one of the problems. Write a few sentences about how you solved it.

Whole-Number Operations

Think, Talk, and Write

Your Turn
Read the problem. Draw a line to the operation box. Show your work in the box and solve the problem.

1. Waiters served 76 bowls of soup and 52 salads at lunch. How many fewer salads were served than bowls of soup?

2. Fifty students play sports after school. How many teams of 8 can the coach make? How many students are left over?

3. A science class works in groups today. There are 7 groups of 4 students. How many students are in the class?

4. Today, 154 adults and 58 children ride the train. What is the total number of people on the train?

Add
Answer: _____

Subtract
Answer: _____

Multiply
Answer: _____

Divide
Answer: _____

Talk and Write About It
Complete the sentences about the story problems.

Vocabulary

| whole numbers | difference | remainder | plus |
| operations | sum | quotient | product |

5. To solve the problems, I used four math _____.

6. The answer to the addition problem is called the _____.

Produce Language
Use math terms to write about how to solve problems. Use your vocabulary cards for support.

Lesson 6

Factors and Multiples

Essential Question How do you explain factors and multiples?

You Will
- Use models to show factors and multiples.
- Learn the difference between prime and composite numbers.
- Use math vocabulary to talk about factors and multiples.

Talk About It

Rate these mathematical terms according to the following scale:

1. I do not know this term.
2. I have heard this term, but I do not know how to use it in math.
3. I understand this term and know how to use it in math.

_____ factor   _____ even number
_____ divisible   _____ odd number
_____ multiple   _____ array
_____ prime number   _____ row
_____ composite number _____ column

What do you know about each term? Explain, using the sentence starters for support.

I do not know what … means.
I know … means …
I think … means …

Your Turn

Look at the objectives listed under You Will at the top of the page. Working with a partner, predict what you are going to learn. Use the sentence starter for support.

I am going to learn about …

Factors and Multiples

Vocabulary in Context Picture It!

array

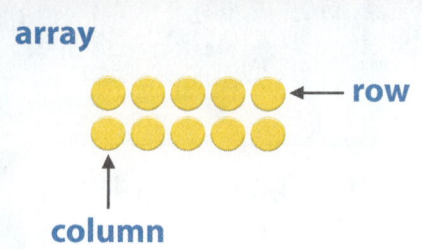 ← row

↑
column

even numbers
2, 4, 6, 8, 10, …

odd numbers
1, 3, 5, 7, 9, …

multiples of 5

5, 10, 15, 20, 25, …

5, 10, 15, 20, 25 are all **divisible** by 5.

factors of 6: 1, 2, 3, 6

$2 \times 3 = 6$ $1 \times 6 = 6$

A **composite number** has more than two factors.
6 is a composite number.

factors of 5: 1, 5

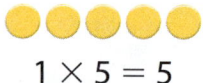

$1 \times 5 = 5$

A **prime number** has exactly two factors, 1 and itself.
5 is a prime number.

Talk About It

Talk with a partner. Complete the sentences.

1. A number with more than two factors is a …
2. A prime number is … only by 1 and itself.
3. The numbers 4, 6, 8, and 10 are all … of 2.
4. The numbers 3, 7, 9, 15, and 19 are all …

Your Turn

Think about the new vocabulary terms that describe numbers. On what date of the month were you born? Describe the kind of number it is. Use as many of the new terms as you can. Share your answers with a partner.

Lesson 7

Do You Understand?

Benito has a sheet of 15 stamps. They are arranged in an array.

① How many stamps are in 1 row? _____

2 rows? _____   3 rows? _____

4 rows? _____   5 rows? _____

② The drawings below show all the different possible arrays for 15 stamps. They can help you find the factors of 15.

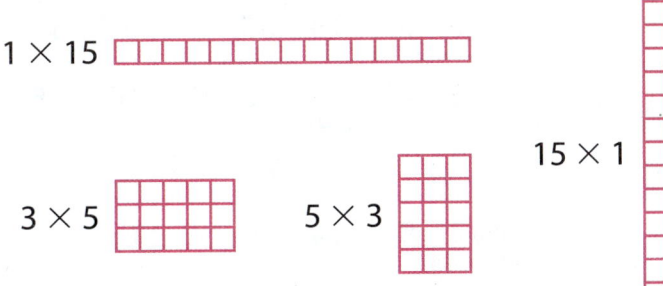

1 × 15

3 × 5   5 × 3   15 × 1

List the factors of 15: _____

③ Use tiles or grid paper to show different possible sheets of 13 stamps.

List the factors of 13: _____

Talk About It

Complete the sentences.

④ The answers to Problem 1 are all … of 3.

⑤ Since 15 has more than two factors, 15 is a …

⑥ Since 13 has exactly 2 factors, 13 is a …

⑦ 13 and 15 are both …

Your Turn

Choose a number between 10 and 20. Write a few sentences to describe that number in different ways. Share your ideas with a partner.

Factors and Multiples

Think, Talk, and Write

Your Turn

A hundred chart is a 10 × 10 array.

1. On the chart, draw
   - **red** ▢ around multiples of 9.
   - **blue** ◯ around ten prime numbers.
   - ✗ on numbers divisible by 11.
   - △ on five composite numbers between 50 and 70.

1	2	3	4	5	6	7	8	9	10
11	12	13	14	15	16	17	18	19	20
21	22	23	24	25	26	27	28	29	30
31	32	33	34	35	36	37	38	39	40
41	42	43	44	45	46	47	48	49	50
51	52	53	54	55	56	57	58	59	60
61	62	63	64	65	66	67	68	69	70
71	72	73	74	75	76	77	78	79	80
81	82	83	84	85	86	87	88	89	90
91	92	93	94	95	96	97	98	99	100

2. How many numbers have ▢?

   _____.

3. How many numbers have ✗?

   _____.

Talk and Write About It

Complete the sentences about factors and multiples.

Vocabulary

factor   composite number   odd number   multiple
divisible   prime number   even number   array

4. The number 74 is an _____.

5. The number 49 is an _____.

6. A number with five factors is a _____.

7. Four is a factor of 28. So 28 is _____ by 4.

Produce Language

Write about what you have learned about ways to describe numbers. Use at least five terms. Also use examples. Use your vocabulary cards for support.

Lesson 7

Decimal Notation

Essential Question What words and symbol should you use to read and write decimals?

You Will
- Use coins and bills to represent decimal place-value concepts.
- Read, name, and write decimals.
- Use math vocabulary to express decimal notation.

Talk About It

Rate these mathematical terms according to the following scale.

① I have never heard of this term before.

② I have heard this term, but I do not know how to use it in math.

③ I understand this term and know how to use it in math.

_____ digit _____ place value
_____ decimal _____ penny
_____ decimal point _____ cent
_____ dollar _____ tenths
_____ dime _____ hundredths

What do you know about each term? Explain, using the sentence starters for support.

I do not know what . . . means.
I think . . . means . . .
I know . . . means . . .

Your Turn

Look at the objectives under You Will at the top of the page. Working with a partner, predict what you are going to learn. Use the sentence starter for support.

I am going to learn about . . .

Vocabulary in Context Picture It!

digit

0 1 2 3 4 5 6 7 8 9

decimal

32.48 — decimal point

dollar 100 cents $1.00

dime 10 cents $0.10

penny 1 cent $0.01

place value

hundreds	tens	ones	.	tenths	hundredths
1	2	3	.	5	4

Talk About It

Talk with a partner to complete the sentences.

1. The dot in a decimal is called the …
2. Pennies are hundredths of a …
3. A tenth of a dollar is the same as a …
4. The number 2.04 has three …
5. The number 0.58 has an 8 in the … place.

Your Turn

Write about the dollar amount, $6.89. Use as many vocabulary terms as you can. Tell your ideas to a partner.

Lesson 8

Do You Understand?

Write how much money each person has in the place-value chart. Then write the decimal in word form.

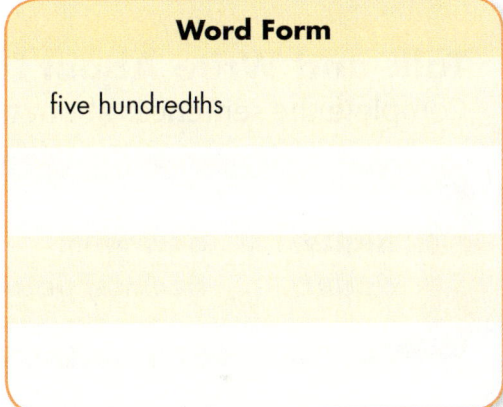

Talk About It
How is money related to decimals? Complete the sentences to explain.

 For both money and decimals, we write a dot called a …

2. A dime is one … of a dollar.

3. A penny is one … of a dollar.

4. $10.12 is the same as 10 dollars and 12 hundredths of another …

Your Turn
Make up three decimals. Use ones, tenths, and hundredths in each number. Write the words you say to read each number aloud. Read your decimals to a partner.

Decimal Notation

Think, Talk, and Write

Your Turn
Finish the signpost. Write each town. Write its distance as a decimal. Use the data below.

Town	Distance in Miles
Arno	three and four tenths
Brilla	eight and seven tenths
Cody	seventy-eight hundredths
Drew	seven and five hundredths
Edna	four and three tenths

Talk and Write About It
Complete the sentences about the decimals you wrote.

Vocabulary

| digits | decimals | tenths | dime |
| dollar | decimal point | hundredths | penny |

1. The numbers I wrote on the signs are called _____.

2. The dot between the ones place and tenths place is called the _____.

3. The decimal for Cody has a 7 in the _____ place.

4. The decimal for Edna has two _____.

Produce Language
Think about how place value helps you understand decimals. Write about how tenths and tens are different. Write about how hundreds and hundredths are different. Draw a place-value chart to help you explain.

Lesson 8

Estimation

Essential Question What vocabulary do you need to understand to discuss estimation?

You Will
- Use place-value concepts to round numbers and money amounts.
- Talk about reasonable and unreasonable estimates.
- Use math vocabulary to discuss estimation.

Talk About It

Look at the list of terms below. In the first two columns of the chart, write terms you **know** or **want** to know more about.

estimate	unreasonable	about
estimation	round	nearest ten
reasonable	nearest hundred	exact

Know	Want	Learned

Tell what you know about each term.

I know the term …
I want to learn …

Your Turn
Look at the objectives listed under You Will. Working with a partner, predict what you are going to learn. Use the sentence starter for support.

I am going to learn about …

Estimation

Vocabulary in Context Picture It!

Estimation is finding **about** how many.
Round to help you **estimate**.

67 → 70
nearest ten

236 → 200
nearest hundred

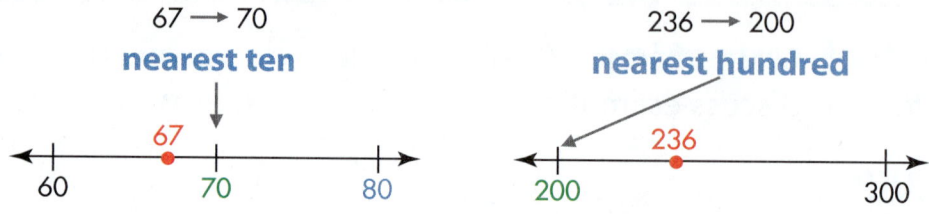

exact price: $36.85
about: $37

exact number: 72
about: 70

$1.25 + $3.88
unreasonable estimate: $2
reasonable estimate: $5

Talk About It
Talk with a partner to complete the sentences.
1. Estimate to find … how many.
2. You can round to help you …
3. The large bone has the … price of $3.88.
4. An estimate that seems about right is …
5. An estimate that seems much too high or low is …

Your Turn
Choose three terms from the chart above. Use your own words to tell your partner what each term means.

Do You Understand?

See what is on sale at the pet store.

   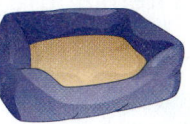

bowl $4.29   leash $9.75   toy $1.77   bed $23.25

Round each price to the nearest dollar.

1. The dog bowl costs about _____.

2. The leash costs about _____.

3. The toy costs about _____.

4. The dog bed costs about _____.

Find each estimate.

5. Two toys costs about _____.

6. You buy a bowl and a leash. You pay about _____.

7. The pet store has 58 dog bowls. About how many is that? Round to the nearest ten.

   About _____ dog bowls

8. The pet store has 217 leashes. About how many is that? Round to the nearest hundred.

   About _____ leashes

Talk About It

What terms help you talk about estimation? Complete the sentences.

9. Round to the nearest dollar to … a price.

10. An estimate close to the exact answer is …

11. If 43 is rounded to 40, it is rounded to the …

Your Turn

Choose any three items pictured above. Estimate the total cost. Talk about your work with your group.

Estimation   35

Think, Talk, and Write

Your Turn
Give each item at the party store an exact price, such as $3.71.

 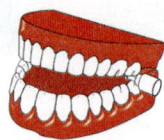  

Mask $ _____   Teeth $ _____   Hat $ _____   Balloon $ _____

Round your prices to the nearest dollar.

1. A mask costs about _____ .
2. Teeth cost about _____ .
3. A hat costs about _____ .
4. A balloon costs about _____ .

Find each estimate.

5. Teeth and a balloon cost about _____ .
6. Last month, the party store sold 575 hats and 238 masks. About how many more hats were sold than masks? Round each number to the nearest hundred. Then subtract.

   About _____ more hats

Talk and Write About It
Complete the sentences about estimation.

Vocabulary

| estimate | round | nearest ten | unreasonable |
| reasonable | about | exact | nearest hundred |

7. Estimation helps you find a _____ answer.
8. An estimate does not give the _____ answer.

Your Turn
Write the terms you learned about in this lesson in the third column of the chart on page 33. Write what you have learned about these terms. Use sentence starters from throughout the lesson for support.

Lesson 9

Fractions and Decimals

Essential Question What words and symbols do you need to understand to work with fractions and decimals?

You Will
- Learn that fractions and decimals can name the same amount.
- Find equivalent fractions and decimals.
- Use math vocabulary to show how fractions and decimals are related.

Talk About It

Rate these mathematical terms according to the following scale.

1. I do not know this term.
2. I have heard this term, but I do not know how to use it in math.
3. I understand this term and know how to use it in math.

_____ decimal	_____ decimal point
_____ fraction	_____ equivalent
_____ mixed number	_____ numerator
_____ number line	_____ denominator

Explain what you know about these terms, using the sentence starters.

I do not know what … means.
I think … means …
I know … means …

Your Turn

Look at the objectives listed under You Will. Working with a partner, predict what you are going to learn. Use the sentence starter for support.

I am going to learn about …

Vocabulary in Context Picture It!

fraction

$\frac{3}{5}$ ← numerator
   ← denominator

mixed number

$1\frac{1}{4}$

decimal

0.75
↑
decimal point

Equivalent fractions and decimals name the same amount.

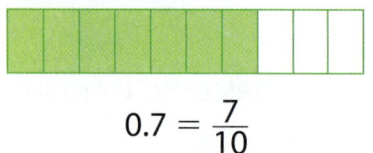

$0.7 = \frac{7}{10}$

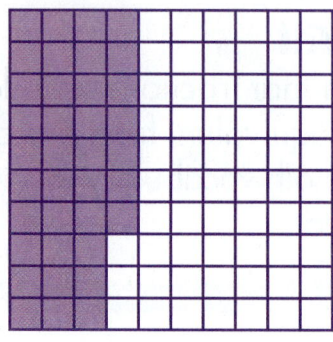

$0.37 = \frac{37}{100}$

number line

```
      0.25  0.5  0.75  1.0  1.25  1.5  1.75  2.0
←——+———+————+————+————+————+————+————+————→
   0   1/4  1/2  3/4   1   1 1/4 1 1/2 1 3/4  2
```

Talk About It

Talk with a partner to complete the sentences.

1. Decimals and fractions that name the same amount are …
2. The top number in a fraction is called the …
3. The bottom number in a fraction is called the …
4. 3.07 is a …
5. $5\frac{1}{2}$ is a …

Your Turn

Look at these numbers: 0.3 and $\frac{3}{10}$.

Use vocabulary terms to tell your partner about these numbers. You may use drawings to support your explanation.

Do You Understand?

The number line shows bus stops. The distances are given in kilometers.

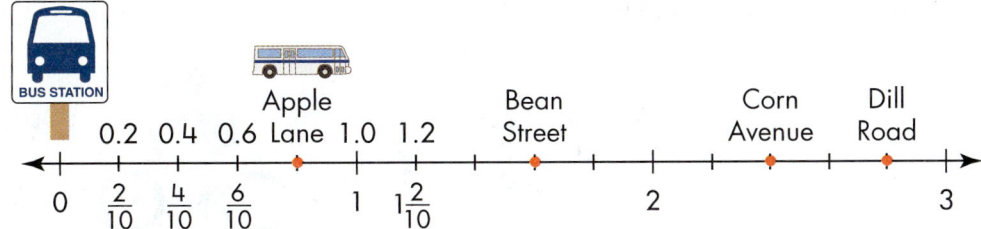

How many kilometers is it from the bus station to each stop? The first one is done for you.

Bus Stop	Fraction	Decimal
Apple Lane	$\frac{8}{10}$ or $\frac{4}{5}$ km	0.8 km
Bean Street	km	km
Corn Avenue	km	km
Dill Road	km	km

Talk About It

What terms help you describe fractions and decimals? Complete the sentences to explain.

1. The dot in 2.6 is called the …
2. The decimal 3.5 and the mixed number $3\frac{1}{2}$ are …
3. In the fraction $\frac{2}{10}$, 2 is the …
4. In the fraction $\frac{7}{8}$, 8 is the …

Your Turn

Look in the box. Two numbers name the same amount. Circle them both. Use vocabulary terms to write about these numbers. Share your work with your group.

$2\frac{50}{100}$ 2.14

$2\frac{3}{4}$ 2.25

$2\frac{2}{5}$ 2.50

Fractions and Decimals

Think, Talk, and Write

Your Turn
The numbers along this bicycle path stand for distances in miles. Write the missing fraction or decimal in each box.

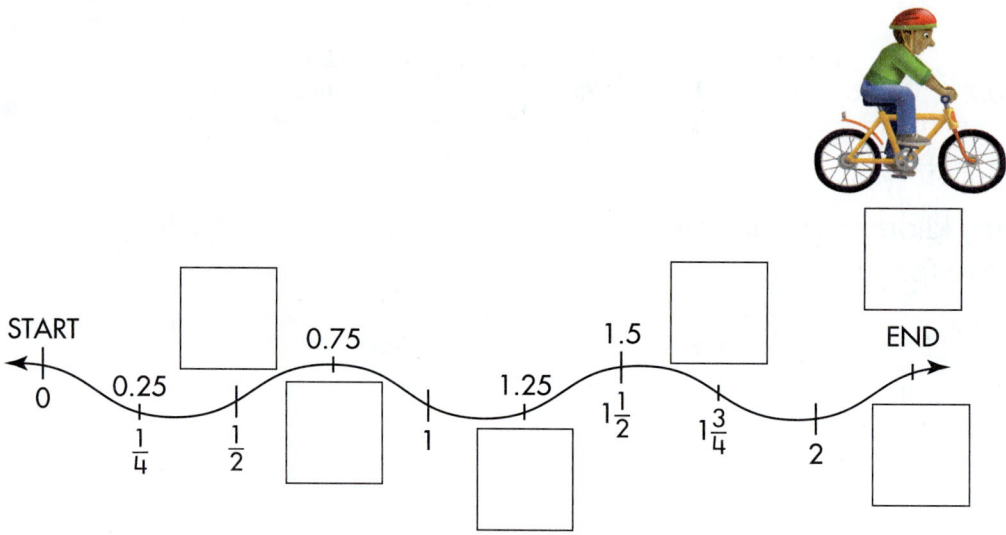

Talk and Write About It
Complete the sentences about fractions and decimals.

Vocabulary: fraction, mixed number, denominator, equivalent, decimal, number line, numerator, decimal point

1. Numbers can be shown in order along a _____ .

2. In the fraction $\frac{2}{3}$, the 3 is the _____ .

3. $5\frac{1}{3}$ is a _____ .

4. 0.75 and $\frac{3}{4}$ are _____ .

Produce Language
Write about how fractions and decimals can name the same amount. Give examples on a number line or use the bicycle path pictured above. Use as many vocabulary terms as you can.

Lesson 10

Patterns

Essential Question What words will help you explain patterns?

You Will
- Understand repeating patterns.
- Understand addition, subtraction, multiplication, and division patterns.
- Use math vocabulary to describe and continue patterns.

Talk About It

Make an index card for each vocabulary term below. Place each card in one of three piles.

Pile 1: I know what this terms means.
Pile 2: I have heard of this term, but I am not sure how it is used in math.
Pile 3: I have not heard of this term.

pattern
repeating pattern
addition pattern
division pattern
repeat
subtraction pattern
rule
multiplication pattern

What do you know about each term? Explain, using the sentence starters for support.

I know … means …
I think … means …
I do not know what … means.

Your Turn

Look at the objectives under You Will at the top of the page. Working with a partner, predict what you are going to learn. Use the sentence starter for support.

I am going to learn about …

Vocabulary in Context Picture It!

patterns

repeating patterns

repeat

1, 2, 3, 4, 1, 2, 3, 4, 1, 2, 3, 4

addition pattern

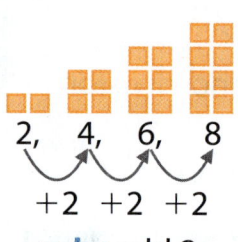

2, 4, 6, 8
+2 +2 +2

rule: add 2

subtraction pattern

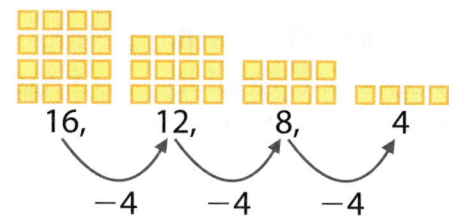

16, 12, 8, 4
−4 −4 −4

rule: subtract 4

multiplication pattern

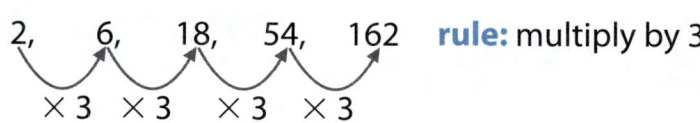

2, 6, 18, 54, 162
×3 ×3 ×3 ×3

rule: multiply by 3

division pattern

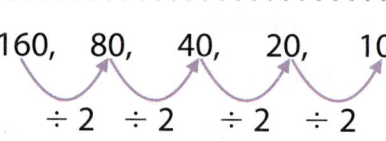

160, 80, 40, 20, 10
÷2 ÷2 ÷2 ÷2

rule: divide by 2

Talk About It
Talk with a partner. Complete the sentences.

 The pattern 6, 2, 5, 6, 2, 5, 6, 2, 5 is called a …

② In the pattern in Problem 1, the first three numbers …

③ In the pattern 3, 6, 9, 12, 15, the … is "add 3."

④ A pattern with the rule "subtract 2" is a …

⑤ A pattern with the rule "multiply by 5" is a …

Your Turn
Write or draw an example of a repeating pattern. Then write an example of an addition pattern. Talk about your patterns with a partner.

Do You Understand?

1. What is the pattern in the necklace? Start with the red beads. Count how many of each color. Write the pattern with numbers.

_____

Find the rule for these patterns. Then find the next number in the pattern.

2.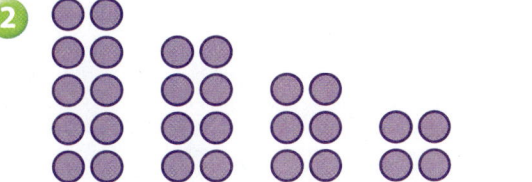
   10,   8,   6,   4, _____

   Rule: _____

3.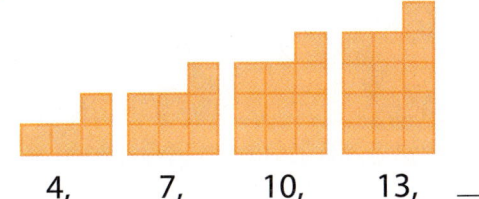
   4,   7,   10,   13, _____

   Rule: _____

4. 55, 50, 45, 40, _____

   Rule: _____

5. 10, 20, 40, 80, _____

   Rule: _____

Talk About It

Complete the sentences about patterns.

6. The pattern made by the necklace is a …

7. The pattern in Problem 2 is a …

8. The pattern in Problem 5 is a …

9. To find the next number in the pattern in Problem 4, I first find the …

Your Turn

Look at this pattern of letters.

A A B C A A B C A A B C A A B C

Write a few sentences about the pattern. Tell what kind of pattern it is. Describe the pattern to your partner.

Patterns

Think, Talk, and Write

Your Turn
Use these shapes to draw a pattern.
Use at least 2 shapes. Use any colors.
Repeat the pattern 3 times.

Write a number pattern. Use any operation (+, −, ×, ÷). Write the rule.

Talk and Write About It
Complete the sentences about patterns.

Vocabulary

| repeating pattern | multiplication pattern | rule |
| subtraction pattern | division pattern | repeat |

1. A pattern that repeats is called a _____ .

2. A division pattern follows a _____ .

3. If the rule is "subtract 6," then it is a _____ .

4. The pattern 2, 4, 8, 16, 32 is a _____ .

Produce Language
Draw or write your own pattern, or choose a pattern from this lesson.
Use vocabulary terms to describe the pattern.

Lesson 11

Patterns in Tables

Essential Question What vocabulary terms will help you explain patterns in tables?

You Will
- Explore number patterns in tables.
- Find the rule and missing numbers in an input/output table.
- Use math vocabulary to discuss patterns in tables.

Talk About It

Look at the list of terms below. In the first two columns of the chart, write terms you **know** or **want** to know more about.

pattern	rule	input
output	table	number pattern

Know	Want	Learned

Tell what you know about each term.

I know the term …
I want to learn …

Your Turn

Look at the objectives under You Will at the top of the page. Working with a partner, predict what you are going to learn. Use the sentence starter for support.

I am going to learn about …

Vocabulary in Context Picture It!

pattern

number pattern

2, 4, 6, 8, 10, 12, …
1, 2, 3, 1, 2, 3, 1, 2, 3, …

table

Number of cars	Number of tires
1	4
2	8
3	12
4	16
5	20

input The number you start with
output The number you get after applying a **rule**

Input	1	2	3	4	5
Output	9	10	11	12	13

Rule: add 8

Talk About It

Talk with a partner to complete the sentences.

1. Numbers and other information can be shown in a …
2. The number you start with in a table is the …
3. What you do to change an input number is the …
4. The number you get after using a rule is the …

Your Turn

Describe the following to your partner. Try to use all of the vocabulary terms.

Number of nickels	Number of pennies
1	5
2	10
3	15
4	20
5	25

Lesson 12

Do You Understand?

Marta is making a floor tile pattern. Every time she puts down 1 hexagon, she puts down 3 triangles around it.

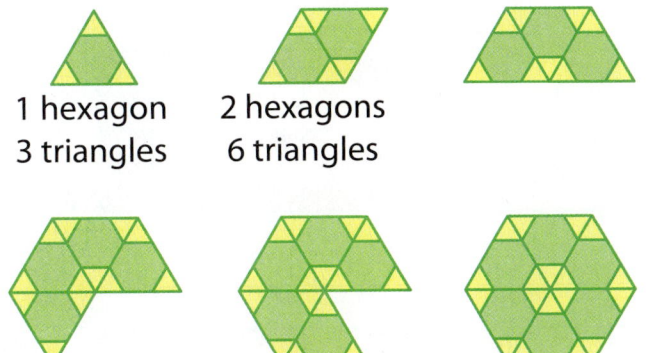

1 hexagon   2 hexagons
3 triangles 6 triangles

Marta uses a table to show the number of hexagons and the number of triangles. Write the missing numbers in the table.

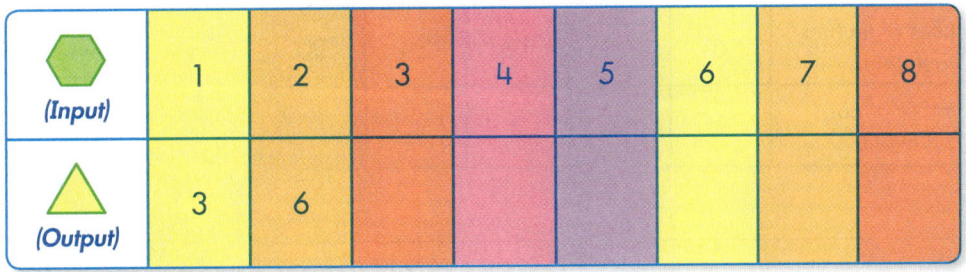

(Input)	1	2	3	4	5	6	7	8
(Output)	3	6						

Talk About It
Complete the sentences.

1. The number of hexagons and the number of triangles is written in a …

2. The number of hexagons is the input, and the number of triangles is the …

3. In this table, "multiply by 3" is the …

Your Turn
Explain to your partner how you could find the next four input and output numbers in the table.

Patterns in Tables

Think, Talk, and Write

Your Turn
Look for a pattern in each table. Write the rule and fill in the missing numbers.

1

Number of weeks (Input)	1	2	3	4	5
Number of days (Output)	7	14	21		

Rule: _____

2

Sean's age in years (Input)	8	9	10	11	12
Anna's age in years (Output)	5	6	7		

Rule: _____

3

Number of muffins (Input)	6	12	18	24	30
Number of bags (Output)	1	2	3		

Rule: _____

Talk and Write About It
Complete the sentences about tables and patterns.

Vocabulary

| output | input | rule | table |
| pattern | number pattern | | |

4 Input and output numbers can be shown in a _____ .

5 The number you start with is the _____ .

6 You change the input by using a _____ .

7 After you use a rule, the number you get is the _____ .

Your Turn
Write the terms you learned about in this lesson in the third column of the chart on page 45. Write what you have learned about these terms. Use sentence starters from throughout the lesson for support.

Lesson 12

Variables and Equations

Essential Question What words and symbols should you use when you work with equations and variables?

You Will
- Understand and discuss what variables and equations are.
- Solve equations with missing numbers.
- Use math vocabulary to describe variables and equations.

Talk About It

Rate these mathematical terms according to the following scale:

1. I do not know this term.
2. I have heard this term, but I do not know how to use it in math.
3. I understand this term and know how to use it in math.

_____ variable   _____ equation
_____ is equal to   _____ missing number
_____ inverse operations _____ value
_____ solution   _____ equals
_____ solve   _____ equal sign

Use the sentence starters to talk about the terms.

I know … means …
I think … means …
I do not know what … means.

Your Turn

Look at the objectives under You Will at the top of the page. Working with a partner, predict what you are going to learn. Use the sentence starter for support.

I am going to learn about …

Vocabulary in Context Picture It!

equation
10 + 8 = 18
↑
equal sign

equals
is equal to
10 + 8 = 18

inverse operations
+ and −   × and ÷
10 + 8 = 18   5 × 7 = 35
18 − 8 = 10   35 ÷ 7 = 5

solve Find the **value** of the **missing number**.
☐ + 32 = 40
☐ = 8 ← **solution**

variable
38 − ☐ = 18   38 − a = 18

Talk About It

Talk with a partner. Complete the sentences.

1. You can say that 3 × 6 = 18 is a number sentence or an …
2. You can use a shape or letter for the …
3. Addition and subtraction are …
4. The answer to an equation is the …
5. In $n \times 42 = 126$, n is the …

Your Turn

Think about the new vocabulary terms.

- Write an addition equation. Use a as the variable.
- Have your partner solve your equation.
- Use vocabulary terms to discuss your partner's work.

Lesson 13

Do You Understand?

Use equations to solve the problems.

1 Each van has the same number of students. How many students are in each van?

24 students in all

What number do you need to find?

_____

The equation for this problem is 3 × ☐ = 24

The value of ☐ is _____ .

There are _____ students in each van.

33 boys and ? girls

2 There are 57 students in this group. 33 are boys. How many are girls?

What number do you need to find?

_____

The equation for this problem is $33 + g = 57$

The value of g is _____ .

There are _____ girls.

57 students in all

Talk About It

Complete the sentences about solving equations. Discuss your answers with a partner.

3 Multiplication and division are … operations.

4 You can show a missing number with a …

5 You solve an equation by finding the … of the variable.

Your Turn

Explain how you can use inverse operations to solve one of the equations above. Use the sentence starters for help.

The operation in the equation is …
The inverse operation is …
To solve the equation, I …

Variables and Equations 51

Think, Talk, and Write

Your Turn
Use a variable to solve the problem. How many pencils are in the box?

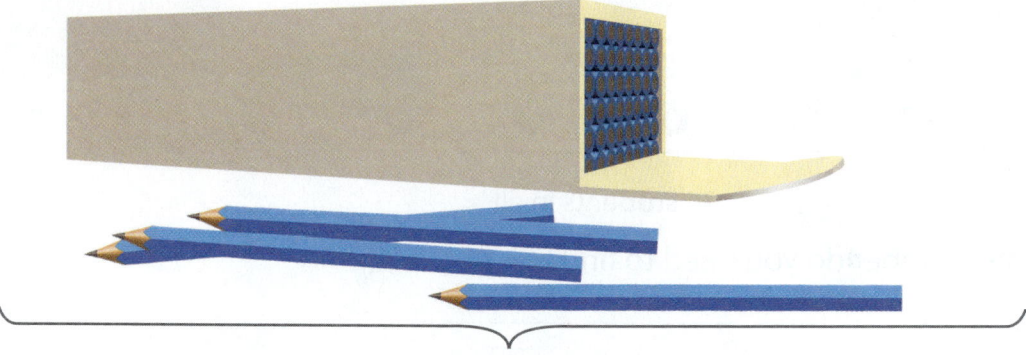

52 pencils in all

What number do you need to find?
_____

Write an equation for this problem. In your equation, use *p* for the number of pencils in the box.
_____

The value of *p* is _____ .

There are _____ pencils in the box.

Talk and Write About It

Complete the sentences about equations.

Vocabulary
variable   missing number   equation   solution
solve   inverse operations   value   equal sign

1. $117 - z = 65$ is an _____ .

2. In an equation, a letter is a _____ .

3. When you find the value of the variable, you _____ the equation.

4. The answer to an equation is the _____ .

Produce Language

Write about how to solve $n - 8 = 16$. Show the steps to follow. Use vocabulary terms. Use Vocabulary in Context Picture It! for support.

Lines and Angles

Essential Question What vocabulary terms should you use to describe lines and angles?

You Will
- Recognize the properties of lines and angles.
- Recognize special angles and special pairs of lines.
- Use math vocabulary to describe lines and angles.

Talk About It

Rate these mathematical terms according to the following scale.

1. I have never heard of this term before.
2. I have heard this term, but I do not know how to use it in math.
3. I understand this term and know how to use it in math.

_____ line   _____ ray
_____ intersecting lines   _____ point
_____ line segment   _____ perpendicular lines
_____ parallel lines   _____ vertex
_____ angle   _____ right angle
_____ acute angle   _____ obtuse angle
_____ straight angle

Explain what you know about each term, using the sentence starters.

I do not know what … means.
I know … means …
I think … means …

Your Turn

Look at the objectives under You Will at the top of the page. Working with a partner, predict what you are going to learn. Use the sentence starter for support.

I am going to learn about …

Vocabulary in Context Picture It!

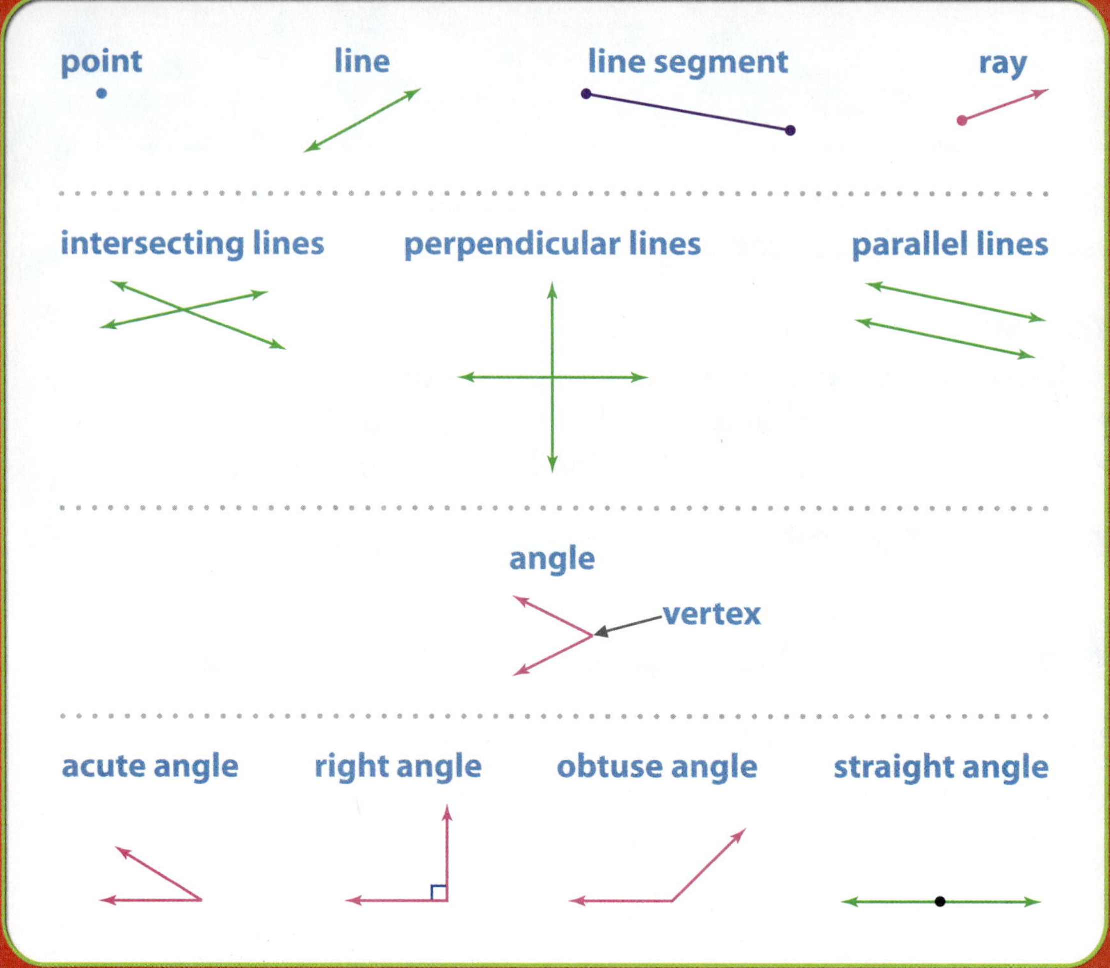

point · line ↗ line segment •—• ray •→

intersecting lines ✕ perpendicular lines ✛ parallel lines ⇉

angle ⟨ ← vertex

acute angle   right angle   obtuse angle   straight angle

Talk About It
Talk with a partner. Complete the sentences.
1. A part of a line that goes on in only one direction is a …
2. An angle that is open less than a right angle is an …
3. Lines that never cross are …
4. Two lines that intersect at right angles are …
5. The point where two rays meet to form an angle is the …

Your Turn
Choose two terms on this page. Draw three different examples of each. Show your drawings to a partner. Ask your partner to describe them.

Lesson 14

Do You Understand?

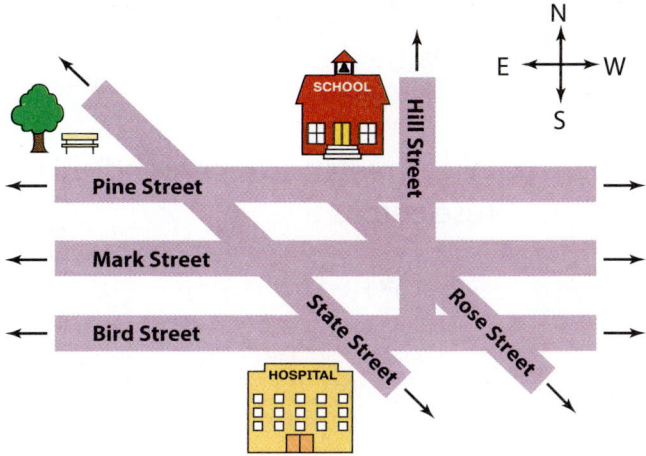

Match each term with what it describes on the map. The first one is done for you.

right angle — Bird Street and Pine Street

parallel lines — The angle where the hospital is

perpendicular lines — The angle where the park is

obtuse angle — The angle where the school is

acute angle — Mark Street and Hill Street

Talk About It

Complete the sentences that describe lines or angles.

1. State Street and Rose Street look like …
2. Where Pine Street and Hill Street intersect is a …
3. Pine Street and Hill Street look like …
4. A line that goes in only one direction is a …

Your Turn

Add to the map.

- Draw a new street parallel to Bird Street.
- Draw a new street perpendicular to Bird Street.

Talk about your work with a partner.

Lines and Angles

Think, Talk, and Write

Your Turn

Draw a street map with 6 streets. Name the streets.

Be sure your map has:
- intersecting streets
- parallel streets
- perpendicular streets
- acute angles
- obtuse angles

Talk to a partner about your map. Use vocabulary terms to point out the special lines and angles in your drawing.

Talk and Write About It

Complete the sentences about your map.

Vocabulary

| parallel lines | intersecting lines | right angles |
| perpendicular lines | lines | obtuse angles |

1. Streets that never cross look like _____ .

2. Streets that cross look like _____ .

3. The angles made by perpendicular lines are _____ .

Produce Language

Identify the kinds of lines and angles you can see in your classroom. Write to describe them. Use Vocabulary in Context Picture It! for support.

Lesson 14

Shapes

Essential Question What vocabulary terms do you use when you discuss shapes?

You Will
- Recognize the attributes of shapes.
- Compare and contrast polygons, quadrilaterals, and triangles.
- Use math vocabulary to describe shapes.

Talk About It

Tear out the Shapes Four Corner Activity sheet on pages 91–92. Then cut out the activity cards on page 93.

Work with a partner.

Each corner of the room shows the name of a shape.

Step 1 Go to a corner of the room. On the activity sheet, write the name of the shape.

Step 2 Look at the shapes on the activity cards. Find 2 cards that match the name of the shape in the box. Paste them in the box.

Repeat Steps 1 and 2 for each corner of the room.

What do you know about the names of the shapes you wrote in each box? Use the sentence starters for support.

I know … means …
I think … means …
I do not know what … means.

Your Turn

Look at the objectives under You Will at the top of the page. Working with a partner, predict what you are going to learn. Use the sentence starter for support.

I am going to learn about …

Shapes 57

Vocabulary in Context Picture It!

Shapes can be **polygons**.

| triangle | quadrilateral | pentagon | hexagon | octagon |

side →
angle →

triangles

| equilateral triangle | isosceles triangle | scalene triangle | right triangle | acute triangle | obtuse triangle |

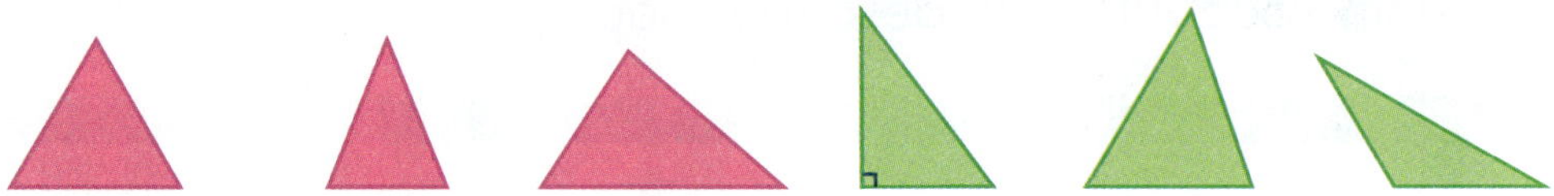

3 equal sides | 2 equal sides | 0 equal sides | 1 right angle | 3 acute angles | 1 obtuse angle

quadrilaterals

| square | rectangle | rhombus | parallelogram | trapezoid |

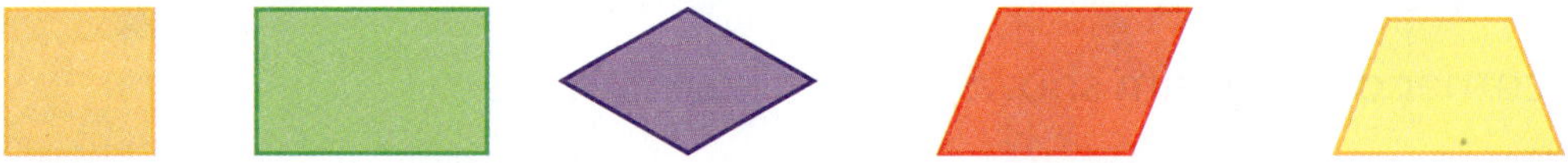

Talk About It
Talk with a partner. Complete the sentences.

1. A triangle has 3 …
2. Any polygon with 4 sides is a …
3. Every quadrilateral with 4 equal sides is a …

Your Turn
Write ways to remember the terms for different figures. List terms that are hard to say. Talk about your ideas in a small group.

Do You Understand?

Work with a partner. Writes as many names as you can for each shape using the vocabulary terms shown on page 58. The example is done for you.

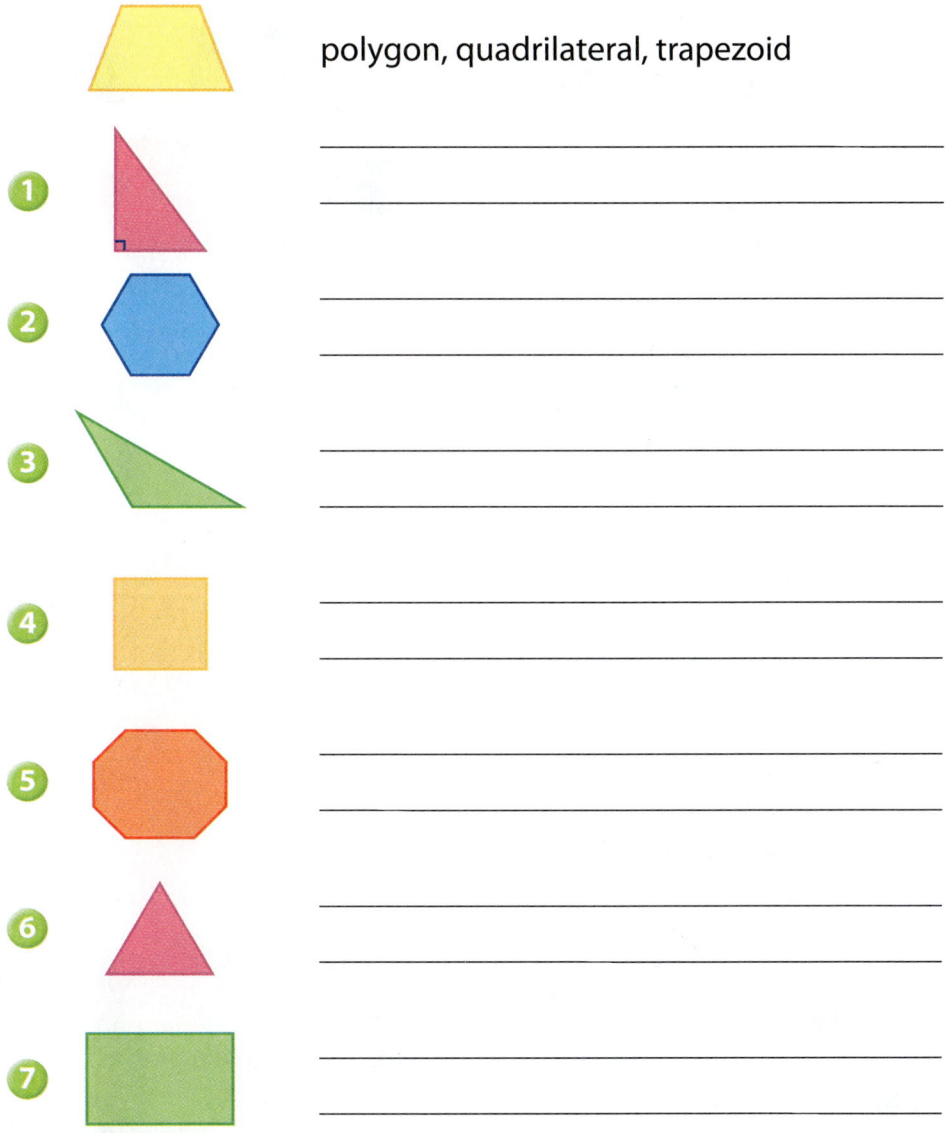

polygon, quadrilateral, trapezoid

1. _____
2. _____
3. _____
4. _____
5. _____
6. _____
7. _____

Talk About It

Complete the sentences that describe figures.

8. Stop signs have 8 sides, so they are …

9. An equilateral triangle has 3 … sides.

10. A polygon with 5 sides is a …

Your Turn

Choose two quadrilaterals. Write how they are alike and how they are different. Draw a picture of each one. Share your work with a partner.

Shapes

Think, Talk, and Write

Your Turn
Design a polygon picture. Draw it on grid paper. Use a ruler to help you draw straight sides. Use at least 7 different shapes. Label the shapes.

Talk and Write About It
Complete the sentences about shapes.

Vocabulary		
isosceles triangle	trapezoid	parallelogram
hexagon	octagon	equilateral triangle
right triangle	rectangle	sides

① A triangle with a right angle is a _____.

② Every polygon has straight _____.

③ A figure with 6 sides is a _____.

④ A triangle with 2 equal sides is an _____.

Produce Language
Write about your polygon picture. Use Vocabulary in Context Picture It! for support.

Lesson 15

Transformations and Symmetry

Essential Question How can you describe transformations and symmetry?

You Will
- Flip, turn, and slide figures.
- Recognize congruence and symmetry.
- Use math vocabulary to describe transformations and symmetry.

Talk About It

Make an index card for each vocabulary term below. Place each card in one of three piles.

Pile 1: I know what this term means.
Pile 2: I have heard this term, but I am not sure how it is used in math.
Pile 3: I have not heard of this term.

reflection	rotation	translation
flip	turn	slide
transformation	symmetry	line of symmetry
congruent		

What do you know about each term? Explain, using the sentence starters for support.

I know … means …
I think … means …
I do not know what … means.

Your Turn

Look at the objectives under You Will at the top of the page. Working with a partner, predict what you are going to learn. Use the sentence starter for support.

I am going to learn about …

Vocabulary in Context Picture It!

Reflections, rotations, and translations are three examples of **transformations.**

flip or **reflection**   **turn** or **rotation**   **slide** or **translation**

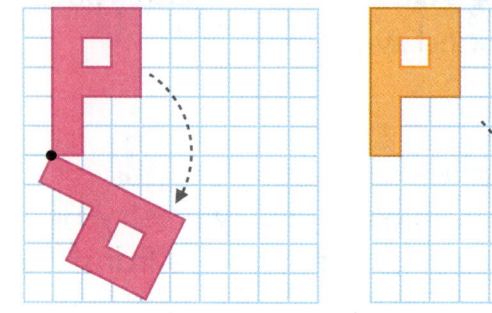

congruent Same size and shape

A figure has **symmetry** if you can fold it in half and both halves are congruent.

lines of symmetry

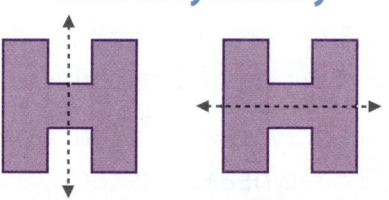

Talk About It
Talk with a partner. Complete the sentences.
1. Figures that are the same size and shape are …
2. Another term for slide is …
3. Another term for rotation is …
4. If halves of a figure match when the figure is folded, the fold is a …

Your Turn
The letter E has one line of symmetry. Draw it. Write how you knew where to draw the line. Tell how to know you are correct.

Lesson 16

Do You Understand?

These letters were made with connecting squares. Here are L, P, J, and F.

L

P

J

F

Write the transformation that was used to move each letter.

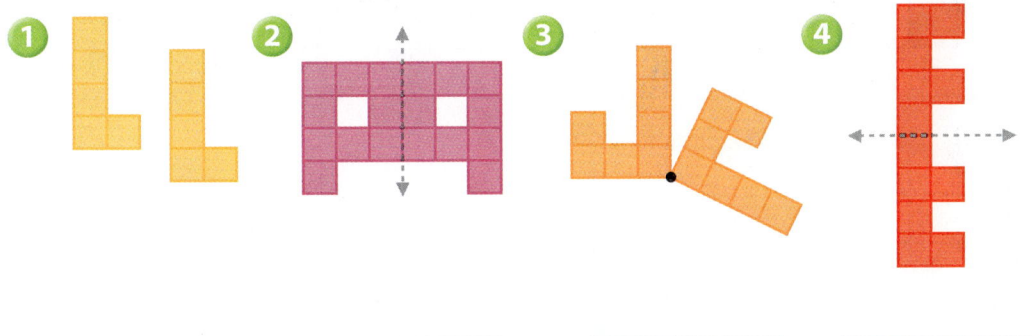

① _____ ② _____ ③ _____ ④ _____

Look at the transformation of each letter.

⑤ What changed? _____

⑥ What stayed the same? _____

⑦ The letter before the transformation and the letter after the

transformation are _____ .

Talk About It
Complete the sentences about transformations and symmetry.

⑧ Another term for a flip is a …

⑨ Both halves of a symmetric figure are …

⑩ Reflections, rotations, and translations are examples of …

Your Turn
Tear out the grid paper on page 95. Write your initials in capital letters. Draw and label three transformations of each letter. Use vocabulary terms to describe what you did.

Transformations and Symmetry

Think, Talk, and Write

Your Turn

"Mirror" is a reflection game. Get a partner and a pencil.

Each player uses one side of the "mirror."

Work together to make a symmetric **M.**

Take turns. Fill in a square on your side. Then your partner fills in the square on the other side to make a reflection.

Two reflections are shown in blue to help you get started.

MIRROR

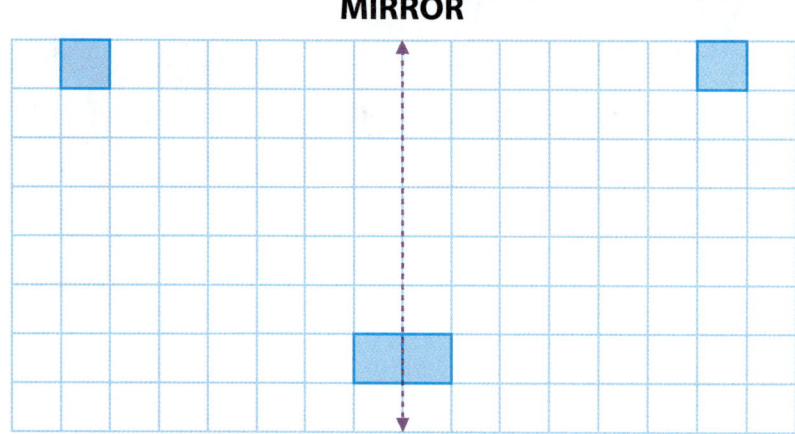

Talk and Write About It

Complete the sentences about transformations and symmetry.

Vocabulary

| reflection | rotation | translation | flip |
| transformation | congruent | line of symmetry | turn |

1. Both sides of a symmetric figure are _____ .

2. Moving figures are _____ .

3. Another term for *turn* is _____ .

4. The purple line in "Mirror" is a _____ .

Produce Language

Write to tell what you have learned about transformations and symmetry. Use as many vocabulary terms as you can.

Lesson 16

Measurement

Essential Question What vocabulary terms should you use to discuss measurement?

You Will
- Understand how to measure length, weight, and mass.
- Learn about measurement tools and some units of measure.
- Use math vocabulary to describe measurement concepts.

Talk About It

Rate these mathematical terms according to the following scale.

1. I have never heard of this term before.
2. I have heard this term, but I do not know how to use it in math.
3. I understand this term and know how to use it in math.

_____ length	_____ ruler	_____ yardstick
_____ mass	_____ pan balance	_____ metric units
_____ inch (in.)	_____ customary units	_____ meter (m)
_____ foot (ft)	_____ ounce (oz)	_____ centimeter (cm)
_____ pound (lb)	_____ weight	_____ gram (g)
_____ kilogram (kg)	_____ yard (yd)	_____ millimeter (mm)
_____ mile (mi)	_____ kilometer (km)	_____ meterstick

What do you know about each term? Explain, using the sentence starters for support.

I do not know what … means.
I think … means …
I know that … means …

Your Turn

Look at the objectives under You Will at the top of the page. Working with a partner, predict what you are going to learn. Use the sentence starter for support.

I am going to learn about …

Vocabulary in Context Picture It!

customary units of length

1 inch (in.)   1 foot (ft)   1 yard (yd)   1 mile (mi) walk in 20 minutes

ruler

yardstick

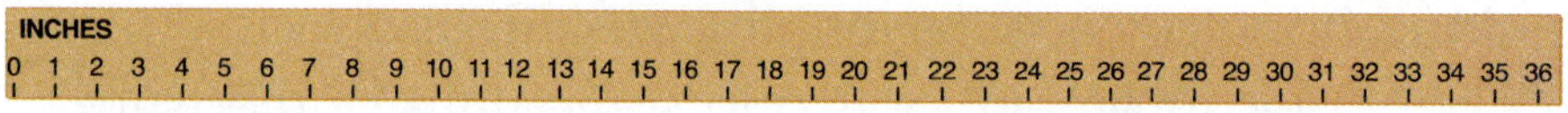

metric units of length

1 millimeter (mm)   1 centimeter (cm)   1 meter (m)   1 kilometer (km) a little over half a mile

meterstick

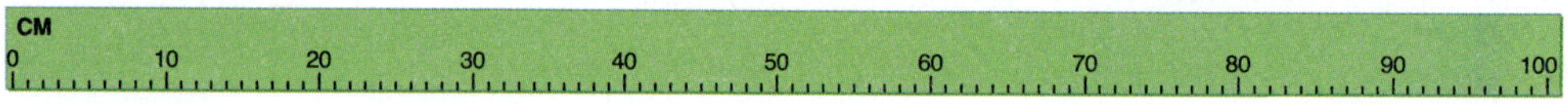

customary units of weight
1 ounce (oz)   1 pound (lb)   1 ton (T)

metric units of mass
1 gram (g)   1 kilogram (kg)

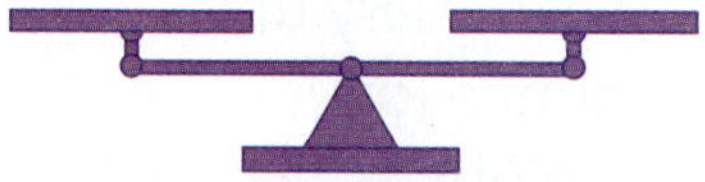

pan balance

Talk About It

Talk with a partner. Complete the sentences.

1. Use a ruler to measure …
2. Use a pan balance to measure mass or …
3. A 4th-grade student might be 5 … tall.

Your Turn

What units of measure and measurement tools do you use at home? How do you use them? Write your ideas. Share them in a small group.

Lesson 17

Do You Understand?

The unit of measure used by the pan balance is _____ .

The pan balance is measuring the _____ of a nickel.

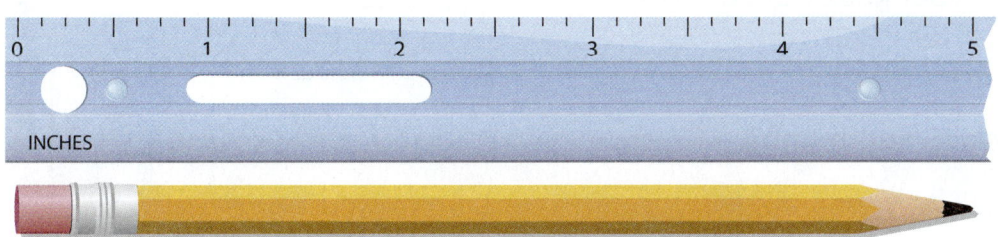

The unit of measure used by the ruler is _____ .

The ruler is measuring the _____ of the pencil.

Measure these objects: your pen or pencil, an eraser, your book, and a piece of paper. Tell whether you are measuring length or weight, what tool you are using, and the unit of measure.

Talk About It
Complete the sentences about measurement.

1. You measure weight on a …
2. Distances on a road map will probably show miles or …
3. Metric units of mass include grams and …
4. The term for how heavy you are is your …

Your Turn
Write about using a ruler or meterstick to measure length. Use as many vocabulary terms as you can. Talk about your ideas with a partner.

Measurement

Think, Talk, and Write

Your Turn
Work with a partner. Help each other measure using both customary and metric units.

How long is your ear? _____

How long is your arm? _____

How long is your shoe? _____

How long is your foot? _____

How far is your knee from the floor? _____

How long is your thumb? _____

How thick is your thumb? _____

How wide is your smile? _____

How long is your arm from elbow to fingertips? _____

How long is your arm from shoulder to elbow? _____

How wide is your hand? _____

How wide is your hand if you stretch it? _____

Talk and Write About It
Complete the sentences about measurement.

Vocabulary

mass	pounds	grams	pan balance
ounces	centimeters	weight	inches
miles	kilometers	length	yards

1. You might weigh a large animal in _____ or tons.

2. A thumb might be 2 _____ thick.

3. A pan balance measures weight or _____ .

Produce Language
Write what you learned about measurement. Tell about measuring yourself. Use sentence starters from throughout the lesson for support.

Converting Units of Measure

Essential Question How can you use vocabulary terms to talk about converting units of measure?

You Will
- Convert customary units of length and weight.
- Convert metric units of length and mass.
- Use math vocabulary to describe measurement concepts.

Talk About It

Copy each term from Vocabulary in Context on a card. As your teacher reads each term, create three piles of cards.

1. Place terms that you know in **Pile 1.**
2. Place terms that you have heard but are not sure what they mean in **Pile 2.**
3. Place terms that you do not know in **Pile 3.**

What do you know about each term? Explain, using the sentence starters for support.

I know … means …
I think … means …
I do not know what … means.

Your Turn

Look at the objectives under You Will at the top of the page. Working with a partner, predict what you are going to learn. Use the sentence starter for support.

I am going to learn about …

Vocabulary in Context Picture It!

You can **convert** one **unit of measure** to another.

customary units of **length**

1 **foot** = 12 **inches**

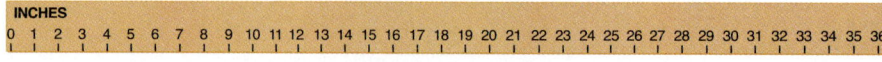

1 **yard** = 36 inches
1 yard = 3 **feet**

metric units of **length**

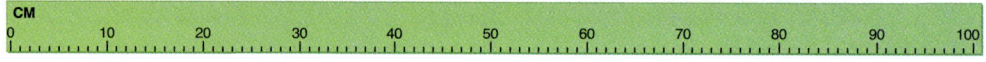

1 **meter** = 100 centimeters

1 **centimeter** = 10 **millimeters**   1 **kilometer** = 1,000 meters

customary units of **weight**

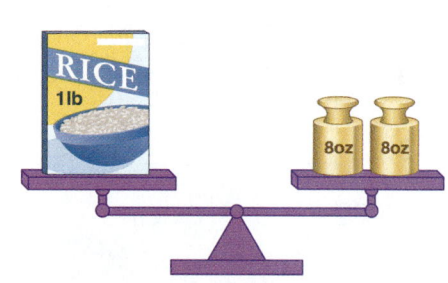

1 **pound** = 16 **ounces**

metric units of **mass**

1 **kilogram** = 1,000 **grams**

Talk About It

Talk with a partner. Complete the sentences.

1. Grams and kilograms are … units of mass.
2. Ounces and pounds are customary units of …
3. Three feet is equal to one …
4. One meter is equal to 100 …

Your Turn

Describe to a partner how you would convert 5 meters to centimeters.

70   Lesson 18

Do You Understand?

Work together to fill in each chart. Include the abbreviations.

Convert Customary Units of Measure
1 foot (ft) = 12 _____
3 feet (ft) = 1 _____
1 yard (yd) = 36 _____
1 pound (lb) = 16 _____

Convert Metric Units of Measure
1 kilogram (kg) = 1,000 _____
1 centimeter (cm) = 10 _____
1 meter (m) = 100 _____
1 kilometer (km) = 1,000 _____

Convert.

1. 12 in. = 1 ft, so 24 in. = _____ .
2. 3 ft = 1 yd, so 12 ft = _____ .
3. 1 lb = 16 oz, so 4 lb = _____ .
4. 1 kg = 1,000 g, so 3 kg = _____ .
5. 100 cm = 1 m, so 600 cm = _____ .
6. 1 cm = 10 mm, so 5 cm = _____ .
7. 1,000 m = 1 km, so 10,000 m = _____ .

Talk About It

Complete the sentences about converting units of measure.

8. One meter equals 100 …
9. I can convert 1 yard to either feet or …
10. 4 kilograms is the same mass as 4,000 …
11. 32 ounces is the same weight as 2 …

Your Turn

Kenji is 5 feet tall. Write about how to convert his height to inches. Tell if Kenji is taller or shorter than 2 yards. Talk about your answer with a partner.

Converting Units of Measure

Think, Talk, and Write

Your Turn
Convert to ounces.

_____oz _____oz _____oz

Convert to feet.

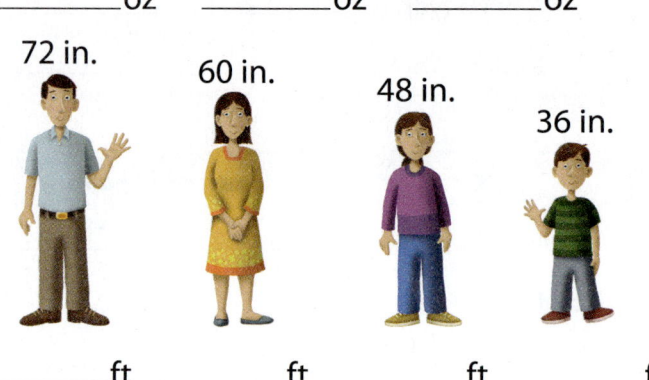

_____ft _____ft _____ft _____ft

Convert to centimeters.

_____cm
_____cm
_____cm

Talk and Write About It
Complete the sentences about units of measure.

Vocabulary

| ounces | feet | inches | pounds |
| kilograms | centimeters | yards | millimeters |

1. One yard is equal to three _____ .

2. You can convert 32 ounces to 2 _____ .

3. 5,000 grams equals 5 _____ .

4. One meter is equal to 1,000 _____ .

Produce Language
Write what you have learned about converting units of measure. Use your vocabulary cards for support.

Lesson 18

Perimeter and Area

Essential Question How do you talk about perimeter and area?

You Will
- Understand perimeter and area.
- Find the perimeter and area of rectangles and irregular figures.
- Use math vocabulary to describe perimeter and area.

Talk About It

Make an index card for each vocabulary term below. Place each card in one of three piles.

Pile 1: I know what this term means.
Pile 2: I have heard this term, but I do not know how to use it in math.
Pile 3: I have not heard this term.

dimensions	irregular figure	square centimeter
square unit	perimeter	width
distance	unit	length
square inch	square meter	square meter
square foot	area	

What do you know about each term? Explain, using the sentence starters for support.

I know that … means …
I think that … means …
I do not know what … means.

Your Turn
Look at the objectives under You Will at the top of the page. Working with a partner, predict what you are going to learn. Use the sentence starter for support.

I am going to learn about … .

Vocabulary in Context Picture It!

perimeter The **distance** around a shape

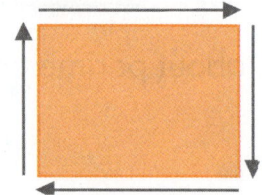

dimensions

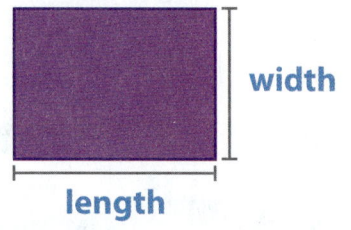

width
length

area The number of square units needed to cover a shape

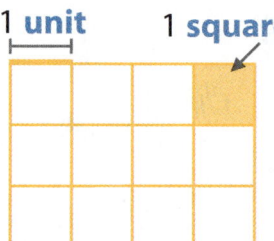

1 **unit**   1 **square unit**

The area of the rectangle is 12 square units.

1 **square centimeter**   1 **square inch**

1 cm
1 cm
1 in.
1 in.

other square units:
square foot
square meter

irregular figure

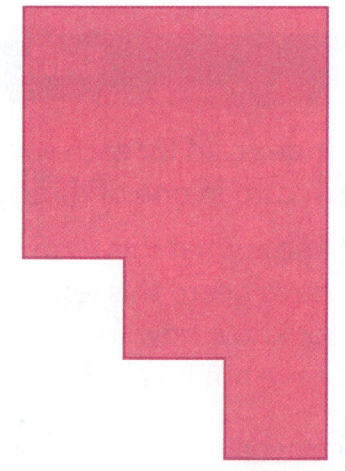

Talk About It

Talk with a partner to complete the sentences.

1. The perimeter of a figure is the … around it.
2. To find the area inside a figure, you can count the …
3. Length and width are two …

Your Turn

Write what perimeter means. Write what area means. Tell a partner about your ideas. Then, explain how you could find the perimeter and area of the top of your desk.

Do You Understand?

Cut out the square tiles on page 97. The drawing below shows the bedroom in a doll house. Cover the bedroom with the tiles. Find the area and perimeter of the bedroom.

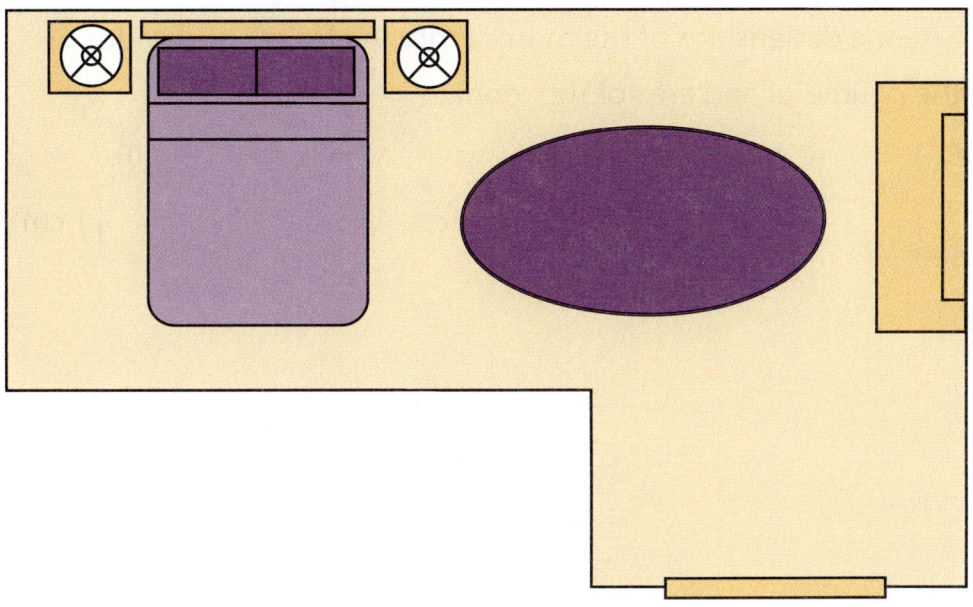

1. Each tile has a length 1 _____ long.

2. The perimeter of the bedroom is _____ .

3. Each tile has an area of 1 _____ .

4. The area of the bedroom is _____ .

5. A figure shaped like the doll house bedroom is an _____ .

Talk About It
Complete the sentences.

6. Measure area using …

7. Perimeter is the … around a figure.

8. A square unit that is smaller than a square inch is a …

9. A square unit that is bigger than a square inch is a …

Your Turn
Make a rectangle out of square tiles. With a partner, take turns telling about the area and perimeter of the rectangle.

Perimeter and Area

Think, Talk, and Write

Your Turn
Draw a doll house room on the grid below.

① Draw a room in the shape of a rectangle.

② What are the dimensions of the room? Write the length and width.

③ Find the perimeter and area of the room.

Talk and Write About It
Complete the sentences about perimeter and area.

Vocabulary

| length | width | area | square unit |
| distance | irregular figure | perimeter | dimensions |

④ The distance around a figure is the _____.

⑤ The number of square units inside a figure is the _____.

⑥ Length and width are two _____.

⑦ A figure that has an L shape is an _____.

Produce Language
Write how to find perimeter and area. Use your vocabulary cards to help you. Draw and label pictures to explain each idea.

76 Lesson 19

Time

Essential Question How do you use vocabulary terms to tell time and talk about the calendar?

You Will
- Read and write time on digital and analog clocks.
- Determine elapsed time.
- Work with the calendar.
- Use math vocabulary to talk about time.

Talk About It

Rate these mathematical terms according to the following scale:

1 I do not know this term.

2 I have heard this term, but I do not know how to use it in math.

3 I understand this term and know how to use it in math.

_____ time	_____ hour	_____ calendar
_____ clock	_____ minute	_____ digital clock
_____ A.M.	_____ day	_____ minute hand
_____ P.M.	_____ date	_____ analog clock
_____ month	_____ week	_____ elapsed time
_____ hour hand	_____ year	

Explain what you know about these terms. Use the sentence starters.

I do not know what … means.
I think that … means …
In math I know that … means …

Your Turn

Look at the objectives under You Will at the top of the page. Working with a partner, predict what you are going to learn. Use the sentence starter for support.

I am going to learn about …

Vocabulary in Context   Picture It!

digital clock   **analog clock**

10:30

hour hand
minute hand

10:30

elapsed time

2 hours 30 minutes

START   END
11:00 A.M.   1:30 P.M.

60 **minutes** = 1 **hour**
24 hours = 1 **day**
365 days = 1 **year**

calendar

days
date
March 8

month

weeks

7 days = 1 week
Sunday, Monday, Tuesday, Wednesday, Thursday, Friday, Saturday

12 months = 1 year
January, February, March, April, May, June, July, August, September, October, November, December

Talk About It

Talk with a partner. Complete the sentences.

1. The clock with hands is called an …
2. You can find dates on a …
3. The time between the start time and the end time is … time.
4. A year has 12 …

Your Turn

Write the time using numbers. Write today's date.

Lesson 20

Do You Understand?

Look at the clock.

- The hour hand is between _____ and _____ .

- The minute hand is on the _____ .

- The time is _____ : _____ .

- It is 20 minutes before _____ .

Answer the questions. Draw the clocks if it will help.

- Use numbers to write the time: 25 minutes after four _____

- Use numbers to write the time: 15 minutes before 11 A.M _____

- A game starts at 2:30. It ends at 4:45. What is the elapsed time?

  _____

Use the calendar.

- January 19 is on a _____ .

- There are _____ Tuesdays in the month shown.

- 2 weeks before January 20 is _____ .

- The date of the last day of the month is _____ .

Talk About It
Complete the sentences.

1. There are 24 hours in one …
2. There are 12 months in one …
3. There are 60 minutes in one …
4. The first day of the week is …
5. The first month of the year is …

Your Turn
Write the time school starts. Write the time school ends. Find the elapsed time in hours and minutes. Share your work with a partner.

Think, Talk, and Write

Your Turn

Use the calendar and clocks to answer the questions.

Field Day STARTS

Field Day ENDS

① The date of Field Day is _____ .

② What day of the week is Field Day? _____

③ What date is 2 weeks and 2 days *before* Field Day? _____

④ What date is the Monday *after* Field Day? _____

⑤ Field Day starts at _____ . Field Day ends at _____ .

The elapsed time for Field Day is _____ .

⑥ Lunch is 2 hours 15 minutes after Field Day starts. What time is lunch? _____

Talk and Write About It

Complete the sentences about time.

Vocabulary

time	month	analog clock	digital clock
year	week	date	calendar
hour	minute	day	hour hand

⑦ There are 7 days in one _____ .

⑧ There are 365 days in one _____ .

⑨ Use a clock to tell _____ .

⑩ You can see days, dates, and weeks on a _____ .

Produce Language

Use vocabulary terms to write a set of instructions telling another student how to use a clock and calendar.

Lesson 20

Collecting and Organizing Data

Essential Question What vocabulary terms will help you discuss ways to collect and organize data?

You Will
- Understand how to collect data.
- Organize data into tables and tally charts.
- Use math vocabulary to describe ways to collect and organize data.

Talk About It

Copy each term from Vocabulary in Context on a card. As your teacher reads each term, create three piles of cards.

1. Place terms that you know in **Pile 1.**
2. Place terms that you have heard but are not sure what they mean in **Pile 2.**
3. Place terms that you do not know in **Pile 3.**

What do you know about each term? Explain, using the sentence starters for support.

I know … means …
I think … means …
I do not know what … means.

data

table

survey

Your Turn

Look at the objectives under You Will at the top of the page. Working with a partner, predict what you are going to learn. Use the sentence starter for support.

I am going to learn about …

Collecting and Organizing Data   81

Vocabulary in Context — Picture It!

survey
Ask a group of people the same question.

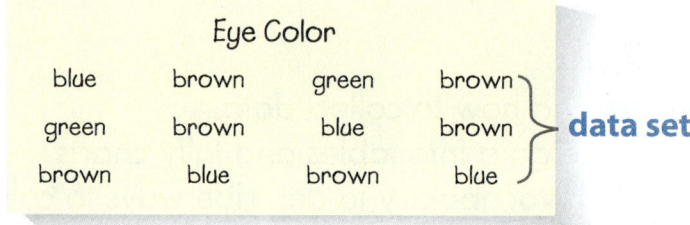

record the **data**

Eye Color

blue	brown	green	brown
green	brown	blue	brown
brown	blue	brown	blue

} **data set**

organize the **data**

tally chart

Eye Color	Tallies
blue	IIII
green	II
brown	IIII I

← **tally marks**

table

Eye Color	Number
blue	4
green	2
brown	6

Talk About It

Talk with a partner. Complete the sentences.

1. People's answers to the question about eye color make up the …
2. A tally chart shows …
3. When I write people's answers to a survey, I … the data.
4. Asking people to name their favorite pet is one way to take a …
5. I write numbers to show data in a …

Your Turn

Look at the tally chart and the table above. Talk about them with a partner. Tell how they are alike and how they are different.

Lesson 21

Do You Understand?

These are the names of soccer players.
The coach wrote their names in a list.
How many names are in the data set?

_____

You can collect and organize data about how long the names are.

First, count the letters in each name.
Then organize data in the tally chart.

Name Length	Tallies
4-letter names	|||||
5-letter names	
6-letter names	
7-letter names	

Finally, display the data in a table.

Name Length	Number of Names
4-letter names	
5-letter names	
6-letter names	
7-letter names	

Talk About It
Complete the sentences.
1. The list of soccer players is a …
2. First I organize the data in a …
3. Then I show the data in a …

Your Turn
What if you join the soccer team? Write your name on the list. Change the tally chart. Change the table. Share your work with a partner.

Collecting and Organizing Data

Think, Talk, and Write

Your Turn

Survey your class to get a list of first names.
How many names are in the data set? _____

① How long are the names? Count the letters in each name. Then organize the data in the tally chart.

② Make a table in the space below to display the data.

Name Length	Tallies
2-letter names	
3-letter names	
4-letter names	
5-letter names	
6-letter names	
7-letter names	
8-letter names	
More than 8 letters	

Talk and Write About It

Complete the sentences about collecting and organizing data.

Vocabulary
organize   table   tally chart   data set
survey   data   tally marks   record

③ I can collect data by taking a _____ .

④ The answers I record are the _____ .

⑤ I write tally marks in a _____ .

⑥ I count the tally marks and put the numbers in a _____ .

Produce Language

Write about collecting data. Tell how you organize data. Use your vocabulary cards for support.

Lesson 21

Representing Data

Essential Question How can you talk about different types of graphs?

You Will
- Understand what graphs are and how they are used.
- Learn to tell one kind of graph from another.
- Use math vocabulary to describe different kinds of graphs.

Talk About It

Look at the list of terms below. In the first two columns of the chart, write terms you **know** or **want** to know more about.

bar graph	labels	symbol	leaf
title	circle graph	stem-and-leaf plot	data
scale	line plot	stem	key
line graph			

Know	Want	Learned

What do you know about each term? Explain, using the sentence starters for support.

I know … means …
I want to know more about …

Your Turn

Look at the objectives under You Will at the top of the page. Working with a partner, predict what you are going to learn. Use the sentence starter for support.

I am going to learn about …

Vocabulary in Context Picture It!

bar graph

Favorite Color ← title

(Number of Students / Color)

scale

line graph

Books Read

(Number of Books / Month)

labels

circle graph

Lemonade (lemon, water, sugar)

line plot

Our Pets ← symbol

Number of Pets

stem-and-leaf-plot

Stem	Leaf
3	2 4 8
4	0 5 5 5 7 9
5	3 4

data

Key: 3 | 2 = 32

Talk About It

Talk with a partner. Complete the sentences.

1. A graph with bars that show data is a …
2. A graph made out of a circle is a …
3. A graph with symbols above a number line is a …
4. A graph with connected line segments is a …

Your Turn

Choose three of the graphs above. Write a sentence about how each graph looks. Talk about your ideas in a small group.

Lesson 22

Do You Understand?

Write which type of graph is shown. Then answer the question.

Student Height (in inches)

Stem	Leaf
4	7 9
5	1 4 4 6 8
6	0 4

Key: 4 | 7 = 47

_____

What is the greatest height?

_____

_____

What fraction of the fruits are pears?

_____

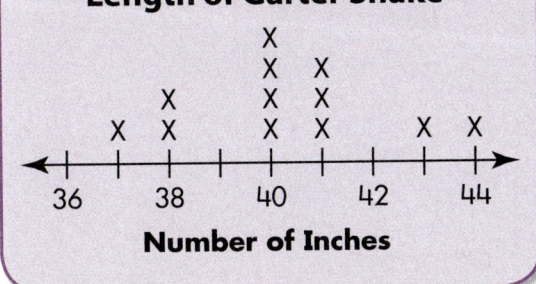

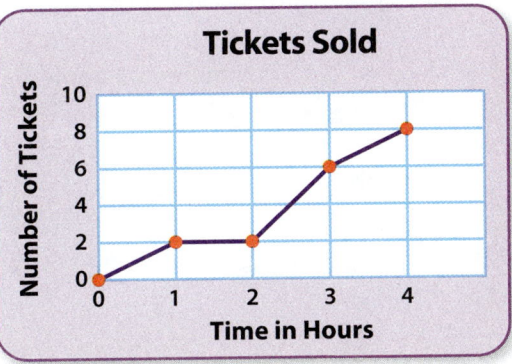

_____

How many snakes are 38 inches?

_____

_____

How many tickets were sold in 3 hours?

_____

Talk About It

Complete the sentences about the graphs.

1. Graphs are used to display …
2. In the first graph, the tens digits are in the …
3. In the circle graph, "Fruits at School" is the …
4. In the last graph, the numbers 0, 2, 4, 6, 8, 10 are the …

Your Turn

Describe the parts of one of the graphs to a partner.

Representing Data   87

Think, Talk, and Write

Your Turn

For each graph, write the type of graph. Then tell your partner a fact about the data.

1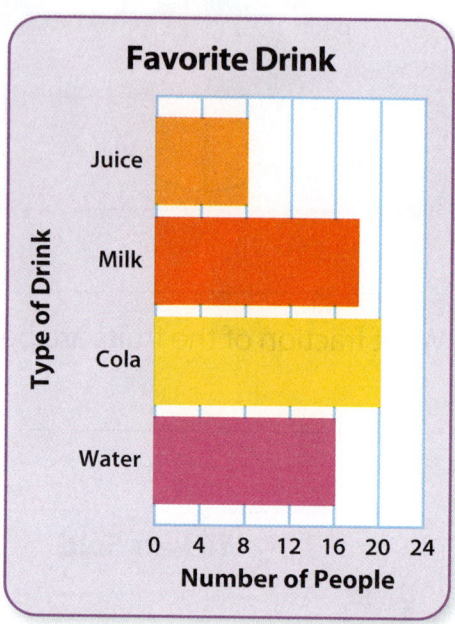

2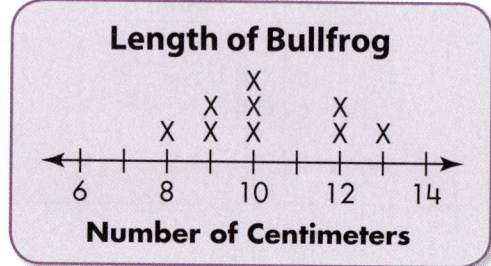

Graph: _____

3

Age of Club Members (in years)

Stem	Leaf
1	8 8 9
2	2 3 3 6 7 8 9 9
3	0 1 1 5 8 8
4	1 3

Key: 1 | 8 = 18

Graph: _____

Graph: _____

Talk and Write About It

Complete the sentences about different kinds of graphs.

Vocabulary

| line plot | display | scale | stem-and-leaf plot |
| key | symbols | line graph | labels |

4 A graph that lists data by tens and ones is a _____.

5 The number labels on the bar graph are the _____.

6 In a line plot, data is graphed using _____.

Produce Language

Write the terms you learned about in this lesson in the third column of the chart on page 85. Then write what you have learned about different kinds of graphs.

Lesson 22

My Addition & Subtraction Words

Addition

add

plus (+)

sum

total

addend

Subtraction

subtract

minus (−)

difference

fewer than

left

My Multiplication & Division Words

Multiplication

multiply

times (✕)

product

factors

array

Division

divide

divided by (÷)

quotient

divisor

dividend

Shapes Four Corners Activity

Corner 1

Shape: _____

Corner 2

Shape: _____

Use with Lesson 15.

Shapes Four Corners Activity

Corner 3

Shape: _____

Corner 4

Shape: _____

Use with Lesson 15.

Shapes Four Corners Activity Cards

Cut out each card. Then follow the directions on page 57.

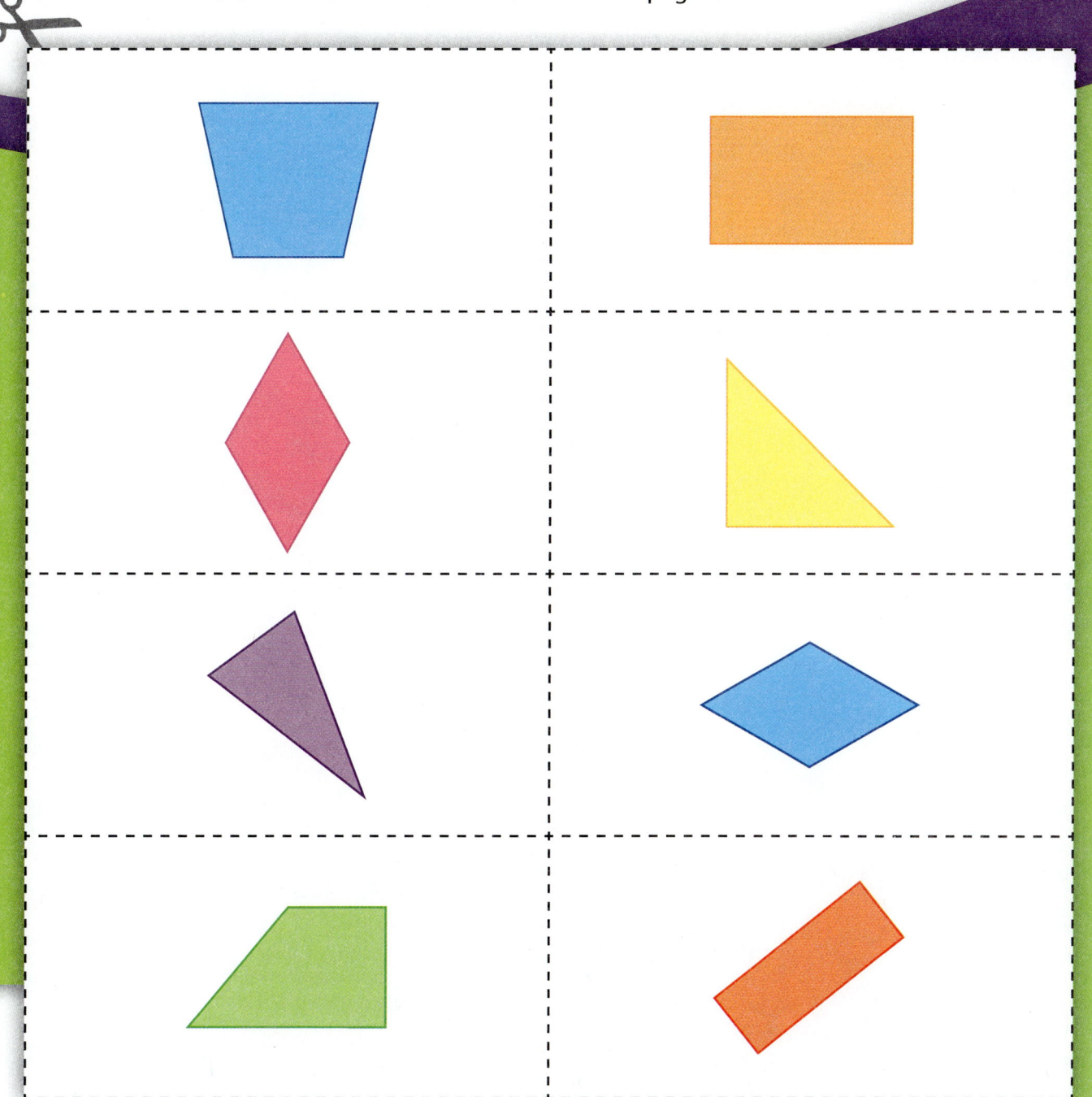

Use with Lesson 15.

Quarter-Inch Grid

Use with Lesson 16.

Inch Tiles

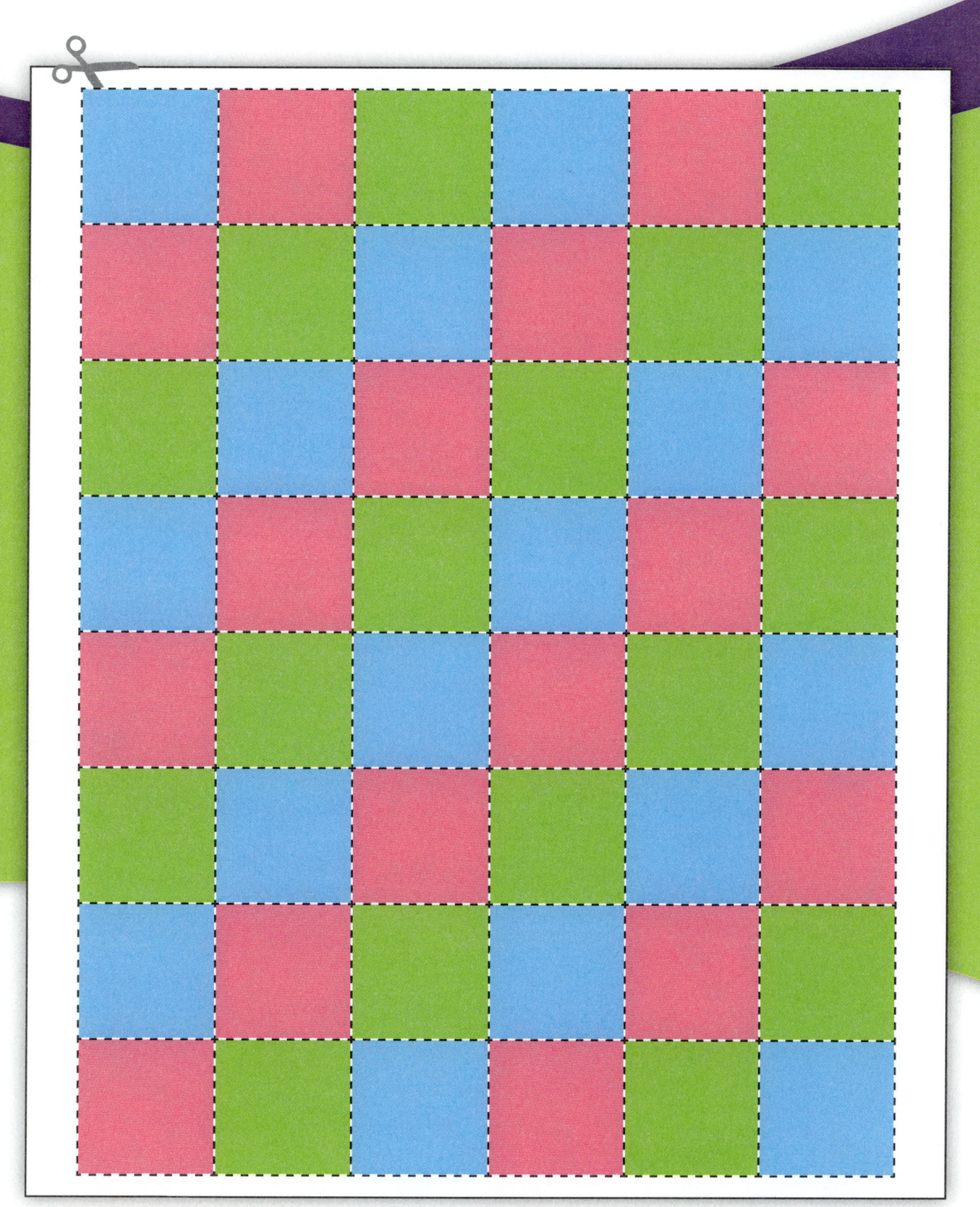

Use with Lesson 19.